This book is unique: it cc
Word with creative work
pastors, musicians, and everyone else who loves to worship God
in the biblical way.

—*Philip Ryken*, *previously senior minister of Tenth Presbyterian*
*Church, Philadelphia, now president of Wheaton College*

For the Christian who has become a bit numb to the grand reali-
ties of God's saving acts recorded in the Bible, Doug O'Donnell's
prescription is a healthy dose of the Songs of Scripture—the
Songs of Moses, Deborah, Hannah, David, and Habakkuk.
This book makes great medicine!

—*Greg Wheatley*, *host of Moody Radio's*
PrimeTime America *and* Sound of Majesty

What a novel idea! Allow the Songs of Scripture to inform
and shape the songs that we Christians sing and, moreover,
how we sing them to the Lord as he is revealed in the Holy
Scriptures. Novel? Yes, and also radical, as Doug O'Donnell
demonstrates: first by uncovering the shared themes of the
principal songs of the Old Covenant (themes also embedded
in the major songs of the New Covenant) and then by using
these themes to analyze the content of today's most popular
classic hymns and contemporary Christian choruses—an exer-
cise that, sadly, reveals their tragic discord with the inspired
lyrics of Scripture.

O'Donnell's faithful expositions of the sacred songs—coupled
with his careful research of current church music, his pointed
analysis of it, and his recommendations to improve it—serve
together to make *God's Lyrics* prophetic. In places (to borrow
Bernini's "Habakkuk and the Angel" image from this book), the

reader will be grasped by the hair and elevated high to heaven, enabled to see life below as it really is.

It is one thing to have the courage to engage in a hard-hitting critique of church hymnody; it is quite another to have the temerity and vulnerability to pen lyrics to fill the void. But O'Donnell has done just that. May his example embolden a gifted new generation of poet-theologian-preachers to help the church sing in concert with the Spirit-breathed Word.

> **—R. Kent Hughes**, *senior pastor emeritus,*
> *College Church in Wheaton*

*God's Lyrics* takes us back to the deeply theological and passionate songs of God's people, graciously preserved for us in Holy Scripture—takes us back to the history of our faith and of the worship of God. We need to know this heritage, which continues to shape how we think and feel and live before God and with one another. *God's Lyrics* helps us understand our present situation and the deep need to worship the Lord with songs and hymns and spiritual songs that extol in explicit and specific ways who God is, what he has done, and how we are to live faithfully before his face. And *God's Lyrics* carries us forward as we seek to pass on to the next generation a glorious tradition of singing that will teach, edify, and encourage our children and our children's children. Doug O'Donnell has carefully and caringly unpacked the treasury of Scripture's songs and provided a rich resource for all who aim to follow along the Bible's own trajectory for worship in song.

> **—Niel Nielson**, *president of Covenant College,*
> *Lookout Mountain, Georgia*

In this timely work, Doug O'Donnell ushers readers into the treasury of biblical music and the world of contemporary Christian music. His sources for the former are five of my favorite hymnic compositions in the Old Testament. Extracting from these texts theological principles that might govern the music of formal worship, O'Donnell offers insightful commentary on the music that drives worship in many churches today. His expositions provide preachers with models of responsible exposition, and his analysis of contemporary trends in music offers musicians a helpful grid through which to evaluate their own ministry. Through it all, O'Donnell pleads for music with integrity that glorifies God and that edifies and transforms his people.

*—Daniel I. Block, Gunther H. Knoedler Professor of Old Testament, Wheaton College*

Irish evangelist John Moxen is correct: Christians who demand truth in the pulpit are often strangely willing to sing lies in their songs. *God's Lyrics* is a sane and salient remedy for this dangerously prevalent condition. As one who prepares over a hundred corporate worship gatherings a year, I am supremely grateful for this practical resource. Doug O'Donnell's compelling expositions and clear applications are well suited, by God's grace, to transform both the Christian worship planner and his people. *God's Lyrics* is a bracing challenge for both classic and contemporary Christian lyricists. It is also a welcome primer, pointing the way forward toward a revival of song texts that are both biblically true and balanced.

*—Randall Gruendyke, chaplain of Taylor University, Upland, Indiana*

I had the privilege of hearing the opening chapters as sermons at College Church in Wheaton, and find that they delightfully and powerfully preserve the preacher's "voice" in print. Here are soul-searching expositions of some of the canticles of the Scripture, the hearing of which creates a longing for something more in our congregational song. The canticle sermons are followed by a search for the biblical themes in the songs and hymns sung by today's church. Here is no style-centered appraisal, pitting new against old, or classic against contemporary. Rather, the lyrical content of some of the most popular hymns and songs of our day is held up to the mirror of the biblical examples. Both sources are found wanting in some respects, and both are celebrated when they measure up.

Doug O'Donnell argues—passionately, humorously, challengingly—that we must compare our singing to the Scripture and take our cues from the Songs of Scripture. And he takes the risk of offering up some of his own texts, based on the canticles he has preached, as examples. May these challenge preachers and musicians to do the same work, and usher in an era of canticle-driven songs for the people of God.

—*Chuck King*, *pastor for worship & music,*
*College Church in Wheaton*

# God's Lyrics

# God's Lyrics

## REDISCOVERING WORSHIP THROUGH OLD TESTAMENT SONGS

## Douglas Sean O'Donnell

**P&R**
P U B L I S H I N G
P.O. BOX 817 • PHILLIPSBURG • NEW JERSEY 08865-0817

Printed in the United States of America

The following songs are quoted with permission:

"Forever," by Chris Tomlin. Copyright © 2001 by worshiptogether.com songs/sixsteps Music. All Rights Reserved. Used By Permission.

"In Christ Alone," by Stuart Townend and Keith Getty. Copyright © 2001 by Thankyou Music. All Rights Reserved. Used By Permission.

"Oh Buddha," by Mark Farrow. Copyright © 1979 by RusTaff Music (Admin. By Dayspring Music, LLC), Dayspring Music, LLC. All Rights Reserved. Used By Permission.

"A Righteous God in Heaven Reigns," by Timothy Dudley-Smith. Copyright © 2006 by Hope Publishing Company. All Rights Reserved. Used By Permission.

"To Heathen Dreams of Human Pride," by Timothy Dudley-Smith. Copyright © 1982, 1984 by Hope Publishing Company. All Rights Reserved. Used By Permission.

"You Are My King," by Billy Foote. Copyright © 1996 by worshiptogether.com. All Rights Reserved. Used By Permission.

**Library of Congress Cataloging-in-Publication Data**

O'Donnell, Douglas Sean, 1972-
  God's lyrics : rediscovering worship through Old Testament songs / Douglas Sean O'Donnell.
      p. cm.
  Includes bibliographical references and indexes.
  ISBN 978-1-59638-172-8 (pbk.)
  1. Hymns--History and criticism. 2. Bible--Use in hymns. 3. Hymns in the Bible.
4. Bible. O.T.--Criticism, interpretation, etc. I. Title.
  BV310.O36 2010
  221.6--dc22
                                    2009053316

To the six pastors
who most shaped my Word-centered
approach to life and ministry:
Ken Carr
Jon Dennis
Randy Gruendyke
David Helm
Kent Hughes
Dick Lucas

You may download original recordings of the six hymns by Douglas O'Donnell, in MP3 format, for free from the *God's Lyrics* page on the P&R Publishing Web site—www.prpbooks.com.

# Contents

# Foreword

THIS BOOK is significant for three different reasons. First, in the first part of the book, O'Donnell develops a biblical theology of the content of God's praise. He exposits a number of significant Old Testament songs and discovers that they have four recurring characteristics (I'll say more about this in a moment). Second, in the next part, he explains what this biblical theology of praise means in practice, by discussing many practical considerations for pastors, worship leaders, and hymn writers. Third, in the appendix, he supplies some factual data on the most frequently sung contemporary worship music and classical hymns, data that take us beyond our subjective hunches and opinions. In addition, in the third part, he presents several examples of his own musical settings for several significant biblical hymns.

In Part One, O'Donnell discovers four characteristics that recur in biblical song:

- The Lord is at the center; that is, our God is addressed, adored, and "enlarged."
- His mighty acts in salvation history (not merely or primarily our personal experience of redemption) are recounted.
- His acts of judgment are rejoiced in.
- His ways of living (practical wisdom) are encouraged.

O'Donnell convincingly argues that these four themes recur not only in the Psalms, but also in the Old Testament songs outside of the Psalter. They become the test by which O'Donnell later evaluates classical hymns and contemporary worship music. Each of the four is fascinating in its own right, but I was especially delighted that his third theme is not merely "judgment," but that God's judgments *are rejoiced in*. Not only the Israelites are called to rejoice in God's acts of judgment; the entire created order is called to do so:

> Let the heavens be glad, and let the earth rejoice;
>> let the sea roar, and all that fills it;
>> let the field exult, and everything in it!
> Then shall all the trees of the forest sing for joy
>> before the Lord, for he comes,
>> for he comes to judge the earth.
> He will judge the world in righteousness,
>> and the peoples in his faithfulness. (Ps. 96:11–13)

> Let the rivers clap their hands;
>> let the hills sing for joy together
> before the Lord, for he comes
>> to judge the earth.
> He will judge the world with righteousness,
>> and the peoples with equity. (Ps. 98:8–9)

The Holy Scriptures are kingdom oriented, and they regard the human race as insurrectionists against God's rule. No king worth his salt will permit such an insurrection to go unchallenged, and the persistent message of the Holy Scriptures is that God has in the past and will in the future remove the insurrectionists from his kingdom, ushering in a realm of peace and blessedness for his people, who are to rejoice with thanksgiving for his mighty acts of valorous judgment in preserving his good realm for them, as they will in the eternal state:

> After this I heard what seemed to be the loud voice of a great multitude in heaven, crying out,
>
> "Hallelujah!
> Salvation and glory and power belong to our God,
>     for his judgments are true and just;
> for he has judged the great prostitute
>     who corrupted the earth with her immorality,
> and has avenged on her the blood of his servants."
>         (Rev. 19:1–2)

Readers will not be surprised that O'Donnell's survey of the most frequently sung contemporary worship music and classical hymns finds that they fail to measure up to the criteria of biblical song, nor will they be surprised that contemporary worship music fails almost utterly. Our intuitive hunch that contemporary worship music centers more on our experience of religion than it does on God's saving acts in history, that in them we as worshippers are more prominent than he who is worshipped, that God's judgment is almost never mentioned in them, and that there is almost no clear ethical guidance in them is substantiated by O'Donnell's survey of the lyrics themselves. As a group (with several notable exceptions, which O'Donnell candidly applauds), the lyrics of most contemporary worship music is only biblical in a biblicistic sense: several scriptural phrases are common enough, but the *general character* of biblical song is replaced by that which is narcissistic, pietistic, sentimental, and Pollyannaish. In such music, the Lion of the tribe of Judah has become a domestic kitten (and declawed at that). He is everyone's friend and no one's enemy; he may elicit our affection, but not our awe.

O'Donnell rightly cites my friend and former colleague, Gordon Fee, who once observed: "Show me a church's songs, and I'll show you their theology." If Gordon is right, then the theology of most churches in the beginning of the third millennium is not the theology of the Bible. The same constituency that purchases Thomas Kincaid's paintings (in which there is a bland paradise without a glorious and morally serious Maker, re-created without the bloody warfare of a suffering Redeemer) not surprisingly sings bland, feel-good music that consistently avoids or evades the utter intractability of our sin, the horror of our Redeemer's suffering, and the certainty of the Divine Warrior vanquishing his foes in the life to come.

Considering his viewpoint, O'Donnell is remarkably even tempered (even lighthearted on occasion) and fair-minded. For example, when traditional hymns are discovered to be defective, he doesn't mind saying so. In my book on a related subject,[1] I attempt to account for the cultural causes of our reaching the present point. What O'Donnell does is provide a biblical theology of the content of praise that may help us do better in the future. Readers who regard Scripture as authoritative, regardless of their current opinions or preferences, will find that O'Donnell makes a compelling case—*tolle, lege!*

Dr. T. David Gordon
Professor of Greek and Religion
Grove City College
Grove City, Pennsylvania

---

1. *Why Johnny Can't Sing Hymns: How Pop Culture Rewrote the Hymnal* (Phillipsburg, NJ: P&R Publishing, 2010).

# Preface

THIS BOOK BEGAN as a series of Sunday school lessons given to the Legacy Class at College Church in Wheaton, Illinois. In thirteen lessons I taught through every imaginable "song" in all of Scripture, including summaries of the Psalms and the Song of Songs. Each class ended with the singing of a new song based on the most central text of that day's lesson, the lyrics of which I wrote. So, for example, when we studied the songs in Revelation, I paraphrased the Song of the Lamb (Rev. 5) and set my original lyrics to a traditional hymn tune.

I so enjoyed this unique endeavor that, when asked by College Church to preach five consecutive Sundays for the morning worship services, these lessons as sermons and these new songs as closing hymns quickly came to mind. Limited to five Sundays, I selected the five songs which best cover the story line of the Bible. So, I preached on the first Song of Moses (which takes us from Abraham to the end of the exodus), the Song of Deborah (from Sinai to the judges), the Song of Hannah (from the judges to the kings), the Song of Habakkuk (from the kings to the prophets), and the Song of the Lamb (from the prophets to our Lord Jesus Christ).

The effect of these messages was more than I had hoped for or had anticipated. A diverse section of people within the congregation as well as outside it (as the sermons were broadcast on the radio and over the Internet)—musicians and nonmusicians, pastors and laity, biblical scholars and new converts, the elderly and teenagers—expressed to me how these sermons helped them to grow in their knowledge of the Bible, faith in Christ, and discernment concerning

Christian music. This book, which is based in part on those sermons, has been written to continue to spread those effects.

Since the first five chapters were originally sermons and are still intended for a broad audience, I have kept some of the language and style of homiletical communication. There are two reasons for this. First, this style makes the necessary scholarly and technical exegetical points of these difficult Old Testament texts more comprehensible.[1] (My work on each passage is not meant to be a critical, verse-by-verse commentary, but rather a summary and application of each biblical text.) Second, the rhetorical effects of personal and pastoral language provide a natural flow to the discourse, which will hopefully better hold the reader's attention.

I wish to thank my colleagues in the ministry at College Church, especially Todd Augustine, Wendell Hawley, Chuck King, and Todd Wilson, for encouraging me to put these ideas into print; and Dan Block, Richard Gieser, Randy Gruendyke, Kent Hughes, Phil Ryken, H. E. Singley, and Greg Wheatley for their strong support of this project. I also thank my good friend, Michael Graves, for his keen insights on the language, history, and theology of these Old Testament texts. Matt Newkirk, Moriah Sharp, and Mark Talbot I thank for their careful review of sections of the manuscript, and Annie Wilson, Hamille Chou, and Emily and Cory Gerdts for their help in research. I also thank Ed Childs for reviewing the hymns and putting them into Finale. My wife, Emily, deserves special mention, for without her insights, her editorial skills, and the constant care she gives to our five children, this book would never have been written.

Douglas O'Donnell<br>
New Covenant Church in Naperville, Illinois<br>
April 2009

1. What K. Lawson Younger Jr. says of the Song of Deborah in his commentary on Judges fits, to some extent, all these biblical texts: "This song poses one of the most difficult passages in the Old Testament." *Judges and Ruth*, NIVAC (Grand Rapids: Zondervan, 2002), 147.

# Abbreviations

| | |
|---|---|
| AB | Anchor Bible |
| ACCS | Ancient Christian Commentary on Scripture |
| ACW | Ancient Christian Writers |
| AOTC | Apollos Old Testament Commentary |
| BCL | Biblical Classics Library |
| BST | Bible Speaks Today |
| *CBQ* | *Catholic Biblical Quarterly* |
| CCC | contemporary Christian choruses |
| CCLI | Christian Copyright Licensing International |
| CH | classic hymns |
| CWS | Classics of Western Spirituality |
| FOB | Focus on the Bible |
| ICC | International Critical Commentary |
| LEC | Library of Early Christianity |
| LXX | Septuagint |
| NAC | New American Commentary |
| NICOT | New International Commentary on the Old Testament |

| | |
|---|---|
| NIGTC | New International Greek Testament Commentary |
| NIVAC | NIV Application Commentary |
| OTL | Old Testament Library |
| PTW | Preaching the Word |
| TOTC | Tyndale Old Testament Commentaries |
| WUNT | Wissenschaftliche Untersuchungen zum Neuen Testament |

# Introduction: A Lost Treasure

YOU WOULDN'T THINK writing ὁ μὴ ἀγαπῶν οὐκ ἔγνω τὸν θεόν, ὅτι ὁ θεὸς ἀγάπη ἐστίν (1 John 4:8)[1] on the blackboard would work, but it did. Every fourth grader in that classroom was captivated as I demonstrated how Martin Luther translated those Greek words into the first German New Testament. Perhaps their captivation was due to my endeavors leading up to the translation, namely, my rendition of Johann Tetzel, as I had each student toss a coin into a coffer to free their souls from Purgatory. Or maybe it was the story of my fourth grade flub, where I confidently answered my teacher's question, "Does anyone know who Martin Luther was?" with an overstretched arm, "Oh, yeah, I know, I know. . . . He was that black guy . . . right?" Wrong. These Protestant students laughed as loudly and intelligently as my own Catholic classmates did twenty-seven years ago. Whatever it was, these ten-year-olds were eating from my hand (the candy in it helped, too).

So as I approached my finale, the likelihood of them rising up and calling me blessed was as probable, in my mind, as their fresh laughter. But then it happened. I would like to blame it on the existence of electricity or on Edison for finding a way

1. "Anyone who does not love does not know God, because God is love."

to control it, for I had kept their attention thus far without any use of it. Yet after I plugged in that CD player and played Luther's most famous hymn, "A Mighty Fortress Is Our God," my expected beatification lost all potential votes.

I wanted to end my little lecture on the life and legacy of Luther by giving them an appreciation for Luther's contribution to church music. So I handed out sheet music and had them listen to a splendid rendition of that tune. I should have stopped there. Instead, I went on to ask, anticipating a positive response, "So, how many of you have sung this before?" No one spoke. No one blinked. An eraser dropped to the floor. "You know, in church," I muttered confusedly. "How many of you have sung 'A Mighty Fortress' in church?" Then I added, in my best everyone-is-doing-it voice, "Just raise your hand."

Reluctantly, to my left, a girl raised her right hand.

"Good," I said.

I was patient now, waiting expectantly for the rest of the dominoes to fall. But there was no movement, no sound. I gave her a grin and a glance, and then, doing what teachers often do when they don't know what to do, I asked an utterly redundant question. "So, does your church sing that sometimes?"

"Yeah, sometimes," she said.

"Good," I said.

I felt, and I'm sure she felt, as if the rest of class had suddenly left the room, called by a surprise fire drill. There alone we faced each other, not knowing what to say or do next. She stared at me with an innocent "Can I go too?" written on her face; I stared at her, attempting to save my face rather than answer hers. Well, I finally made a move. I added a question of curiosity and of seeming importance: "So, what church do you attend?"

"Faith," she coughed. "Lutheran," she concluded.

My grin unglued. "Oh, Faith *Lutheran*," I said. "Good."

One hand—and it was that of a little Lutheran!

We were both embarrassed. She was embarrassed because she was the only one. I was embarrassed because she was the only one. How could she be the only student out of thirty to have ever heard this song—the most enduring and likely the most popular Protestant song of all time? That's what I thought.

The bell rang. The teacher smiled. I smiled. They smiled. I gathered the leftover sheet music, the coffer and coins, the CD. I took my coat and walked to the car and started it. Then my thoughts raced. What's with churches today? If they're not singing "A Mighty Fortress," what songs are they singing? Will these children never sing a Wesley or Watts hymn? Will they never sing "Great Is Thy Faithfulness" or "Come Thou Fount" or "It Is Well with My Soul"? Will they never bellow out "God of Concrete, God of Steel"? (And will they never know my last question was a joke?) Has a whole generation—as represented by these children and their various churches—lost the treasure of classic hymnody?

Now, I know an oldie is not necessarily a goodie. I know a traditional song does not necessarily mean a tasteful or a truthful one. I know that longevity, sentimentality, and popularity are no guarantees of musical merit or lyrical value. But I also know "A Mighty Fortress"—a song based directly on Psalm 46, supported with scriptural quotations and allusions, and filled with Christian themes and theology—is a real treasure, something of unmistakable value both for the Christian soul and the Christian church.[2] What a loss!

2. Robert G. Rayburn noted nearly thirty years ago, "One of the major contributing factors to the superficiality of the lives of evangelical Christians in our country today is the failure of the churches to teach and use the great hymns of the church universal in their services of worship." *O Come, Let Us Worship: Corporate Worship in the Evangelical Church* (Grand Rapids: Baker, 1980), 223.

# Another Lost Treasure

Sadly, this loss is being repeated many times over at an even deeper level in the evangelical church today—not in the abandonment of the great hymns per se, but in the abandonment of the very Songs of Scripture[3]—the six divinely inspired lyrical poems found in the narrative of Scripture's historical and prophetical books. Of course, not every song of and in Scripture has been lost, for the Psalms, the Lucan canticles (the Magnificat and the Nunc Dimittis), and even some of the songs in Revelation (the Sanctus—"Holy, holy, holy") and portions of the Song of Songs have found and retained their place in Christian theology, liturgy, and music. Yet the six songs found in the narrative of the historical and prophetic books are all but absent in Christian worship—the two songs of Moses (Ex. 15 and Deut. 32), the Song of Deborah (Judg. 5), the songs in Samuel (1 Sam. 2:1–10; 2 Sam. 22), and the Song of Habakkuk (Hab. 3).[4] This absence is tragic. It is tragic because not only these biblical texts, but also their themes and theology—which in a unique way put Christ at the center—have virtually disappeared from contemporary congregational song.

This book is an attempt to rediscover this lost treasure, and to dig up and display, if you will, something of the great value of the content of these Songs of Scripture for Christian orthodoxy and doxology.

---

3. Throughout this book, I will capitalize the phrase "Song(s) of Scripture" to reference the six songs of our study. Also, at times, I will use the phrase "scriptural songs" in reference to them.

4. Since the text of 2 Samuel 22 is almost identical with Psalm 18, there are (given the rich history of psalmody) more songs based on this text than the others. Yet none of those songs are popular today.

Two important points will be emphasized. First, these songs are valuable because, by their providential placement within the Christian canon, they provide unique poetic summaries of, and reflections upon, many of the key points of Old Testament salvation history. In this way, just as the Song of Songs might be rightly called a poetic reflection on Genesis 2, and the book of Ecclesiastes a poetic reflection on Genesis 3, so these Songs of Scripture are but a poetic reflection on the story line of the Old Testament—a story line which, with its types and shadows and its patterns and prophecies, comes to a climax in the person and work of our Lord Jesus Christ.

Second, these songs are valuable because they underscore important, yet often neglected, theological truths. That is, they exhort us to be Lord centered in our singing. They remind us to remember and rejoice in God's mighty acts in history, including his just judgments. And they urge us to moral transformation—to grow in godliness or true wisdom.

In the chapters that follow (and the original songs that accompany them),[5] I seek to underscore the value of these points. Part One (chapters 1–5) presents my exegesis of the biblical texts. In chapters 1 and 2, we look at the songs of Moses. After the exodus (Ex. 15) and at the end of the Torah (Deut. 32), two songs enter our canon. Both point us to the greater, future exodus—not only of the cross, but also of Christ's return—where God's judgment will come completely and justly upon all his enemies, and God's people will be fully and finally delivered. In chapter 3, we look at the Song of Deborah. In the time of the judges we see how the two themes of her song—God triumphing in righteousness, and God triumphing through weakness—collide and culminate in

---

5. For each Song of Scripture, I have written new lyrics (mostly paraphrases of the biblical texts), set to old hymn tunes (e.g., LEONI). These are provided in Part Three.

the person and work of Christ—in Christ and him crucified. In chapter 4, we turn our attention to the two songs that bookend the book of Samuel—the Song of Hannah (in 1 Sam. 2:1–10) and the Song of David (in 2 Sam. 22). These songs introduce us to God's anointed—ultimately to David's greater Son, our Lord Jesus Christ. Here we show how God has worked, is working, and will work in fulfilling his plan of judgment and mercy. In chapter 5, we come to the Song of Habakkuk. In Habakkuk's hymn, we will listen to the voice of the prophet—representative of the voices of the prophets—as he waits in faith for God's coming deliverance (his wrath upon evildoers and the salvation of his elect). Again, we will show how Habakkuk's longings are fulfilled in Christ.

Part Two (chapters 6–10) focuses on application. Here we make direct application to songwriting and song singing in the church today,[6] seeking to answer the question: what do these scriptural songs add to our understanding of what should be the lyrical content of our worship songs?[7] Sadly, we will discover that many contemporary and some classic lyrics have blurred our perception of God and his work. By showing characteris-

---

6. Our study is limited to the content of song lyrics, with no comment being made on the important issues of Christian music and musicians (e.g., the relationship between lyrics and melodies or the use of certain instruments). These issues and others like them are very important. Thankfully, there are a number of discerning musicians who have already done excellent work in addressing them, notably Paul S. Jones, *Singing and Making Music* (Phillipsburg, NJ: P&R Publishing, 2006), and Calvin M. Johansson, *Discipling Music Ministry: Twenty-first Century Directions* (Peabody, MA: Hendrickson, 1992). See also, for a broader historical perspective, chapter 12, "Postlude: What Can the Early Church Teach Us about Music?" in Calvin R. Stapert, *A New Song for an Old World: Musical Thought in the Early Church* (Grand Rapids: Eerdmans, 2007), 194–209.

7. I resonate with the question raised by Paul Jones, "Why is it that we preach, teach, and refer to the Bible on all matters spiritual, and yet when we come to consider worship music (a spiritual and biblical activity), we turn to opinion, preference, and limited experience as our allies and sources?" *Singing and Making Music*, 132.

tics of these "sacred songs" (1 Chron. 16:42) within the sacred writings—such as their God-centered yet personal nature, their emphasis on the works of God in salvation history, and especially their joy in judgment—we will offer both a corrective and a call: a corrective to sing lyrics that will not only make us "wise for salvation," but will also be profitable for "training in righteousness" (2 Tim. 3:14–16), as well as a call to return to the Word of God (the very words of God!) in our worship of him.[8]

Our Lord Jesus said, "The kingdom of heaven is like treasure hidden in a field" (Matt. 13:44). My prayer for the contemporary church is that these Songs of Scripture—which enhance what we know of the kingdom of God and of its King—would be rediscovered and recognized as a treasure, a treasure to be opened and accepted by all, by thirty out of thirty fourth graders and by ten thousand out of ten thousand Christian churches.

8. "My tongue will sing of your word" (Ps. 119:172).

# PART ONE

# Sermons on the Songs

Then Moses and the people of Israel sang this song to the
LORD, saying,
  "I will sing to the LORD, for he has triumphed gloriously;
    the horse and his rider he has thrown into the sea.
  ² The LORD is my strength and my song,
    and he has become my salvation;
  this is my God, and I will praise him,
    my father's God, and I will exalt him.
  ³ The LORD is a man of war;
    the LORD is his name.
  ⁴ Pharaoh's chariots and his host he cast into the sea,
    and his chosen officers were sunk in the Red Sea.
  ⁵ The floods covered them;
    they went down into the depths like a stone.
  ⁶ Your right hand, O LORD, glorious in power,
    your right hand, O LORD, shatters the enemy.
  . . . . . . . . . . . . . . . . . . . . . . . . . . . . . . . . .

  ¹¹ Who is like you, O LORD, among the gods?
    Who is like you, majestic in holiness,
    awesome in glorious deeds, doing wonders?
        (Ex. 15:1–6, 11)

# 1

# The Song of Moses: *Te Deum* of Triumph[1]

NEARLY THIRTY YEARS after the signing of the Declaration of Independence, Thomas Jefferson authored *The Life and Morals of Jesus of Nazareth*, now commonly referred to as the Jefferson Bible. This Bible was Jefferson's private declaration of independence, we might say, from historic Christian theology, for he edited out all the parts of the Gospels which didn't fit his deistic theology. Using his naturalistic and rationalistic grid, he removed all supernaturalism, including references to the Trinity, as well as to the divinity, miracles, and resurrection of Jesus. His Bible begins with the birth narrative, minus mention of angels and prophecy, and it concludes with the cross and the tomb (but not an empty one): "There laid they Jesus. And

1. I am indebted to Phil Ryken for this phrase. See Philip Graham Ryken, *Exodus*, PTW (Wheaton, IL: Crossway, 2005), 403.

rolled a great stone to the door of the sepulchre, and departed." Those words from the nineteenth chapter of the gospel of John are the last words we find. Jesus died and was buried—period, end of story.

While we may not be as bold as Jefferson when it comes to what we do with the pages of our Bibles, there is, nevertheless, a bit of his independence in us all. For when we come to a text like this, the Song of Moses, commonly called the "Song of the Sea" in the history of Jewish interpretation, we are tempted to play God with God's Word—to leave in what sounds sensible, and to cut out what doesn't.

So, we can sing verse 1a, "I will sing to the LORD, for he has triumphed gloriously," but not verse 1b, "the horse and his rider he has thrown into the sea." Or we can sing verse 2, "The LORD is my strength and my song, and he has become my salvation; this is my God, and I will praise him, my father's God, and I will exalt him," but certainly not the beginning of verse 3, "The LORD is a man of war." And we can sing the beginning of verse 6, "Your right hand, O LORD, glorious in power," but it's hard for us to finish the thought: "Your right hand, O LORD, shatters the enemy."

And when we come to verse 11 (that wonderful verse!) we can stand and shout, "Who is like you, O LORD, among the gods? Who is like you, majestic in holiness, awesome in glorious deeds, doing wonders?" But do we stay standing when we recall the actual deeds? Those we find in verses 4, 5, 7, 8, 9, 10, 14, 15, and 16—which speak of Pharaoh and his army being "sunk in the Red Sea" (v. 4), and tell us that "the floods covered them" and that their bodies "went down into the depths like a stone" (v. 5). Or what do we do with verse 7? Can we sing, "In the greatness of your majesty you overthrow your adversaries; you send out your fury; it consumes them like stubble"? What about verse 8 ("At the blast of your nostrils the waters piled up; the floods stood up in a heap; the deeps congealed in the heart of the sea") or verse 10 ("You blew with your wind; the sea covered them; they sank like lead in the mighty waters") or verse 12 ("You stretched out your right hand; the earth swallowed them")? Can we sing of God throwing and shattering and casting and consuming?

We can sing verses 13 and 17 and 18, which speak of the Lord's leading his people out of Egypt and into the Promised Land: "You have led in your steadfast love the people whom you have redeemed; you have guided them by your strength to your holy abode" (v. 13). But can we sing what falls between those verses, of the "terror and dread" that will fall upon "the inhabitants of Canaan" as God will uproot the Canaanites in order to plant his people, to set them upon his holy mountain in Jerusalem?

Maybe Jefferson was right!² Maybe this founding father has something to teach us. Maybe we should cut and paste our Bibles, making them a collage of our culture, a mirror of our worldly minds and its conceptions of God and justice and salvation. Maybe we should declare that God's only attribute is niceness, that it is somehow "evil" to punish evil, and that I'm okay and you're okay and God's okay with us being okay. Or maybe we should just cut out all this cutting out and hear what God has to say, and be open to the fact that our perceptions of reality might be wrong,

2. Or maybe the heretic Marcion was right, who sixteen centuries before Jefferson did nearly the identical thing, taking out certain gospels and other parts of Scripture he didn't affirm, and declaring that the God of the Old Testament was a different God than that of the New, the first being a God of wrath and the latter a God of love.

our concepts of justice might be imperfect, our thoughts on God insufficient.

## Walking through the Wardrobe

I don't know if you have read much C. S. Lewis, J. R. R. Tolkien, or George MacDonald, but there is at least one common thread in the writings of these famous writers. That is the notion of journeying from one world to the next—stepping through the wardrobe, if you will—into a world we didn't know exists, but in fact does. With a song like this, which sings of deliverance but also destruction—the parting of the Rea Sea, but also its closing; judgment, but also joy in judgment—we not only need to do a bit of stepping through, but also a bit of climbing back. We need to move from the world and worldview of the Bible back to our world and the way we think. And we need to be willing to mold our minds, and the reality we seemingly see in this world, with a Greater Reality, the truer reality of God's Word and his coming kingdom.

So, what we'll do in this chapter is walk through that wardrobe, taking with us some rope, a few boards or planks, and whatever else we need to build a bridge, a bridge across this conceptual chasm. We will build a bridge so that we might understand why it is right for us to join in the chorus, to sing with Moses, to dance with Miriam, to pound and shake the tambourine along with the generation of the great exodus from Egypt.

## The Greatness of God

The first plank we must lay down and secure in place is a better understanding of the greatness of God.

Whenever I fly in an airplane, I am amazed at how this huge and heavy metal tube filled with hundreds of bodies and hundreds of suitcases lifts off the ground and flies hundreds of miles in the air. I know the basic physics of it. I know how it works. Yet when I'm actually lifted off the ground and I look out the window at those huge engines and straight, hard, metal wings, I think to myself, "Okay. Now, how does all this really work? This is quite unbelievable. What an achievement. We're flying!"

But do you know what I find so ironic about this achievement? Just when I want to stand up in the middle of the plane and shout, "Wow, aren't humans great!" I take a peek out the window at the people on the ground, only a few moments after takeoff, and they look like a bunch of ants. Then, after a few more seconds in the air, even the Sears Tower is but a sliver in the silver sky.

Now, how big do you think we look to the God who created this immense and awesome universe—the heavens (all that is up there and out there) and the earth (all that is down here)? Like ants? No, we're not that big. Like a speck of dust in an ant's eye? No, we're not even that big. Like nothing? No, we're not that small. We are something to God, but so often not what we think. (Of course, all this is what makes the incarnation the most inscrutable act of history—God became a man! How unthinkable, how extraordinary, how beautiful!) We are something to God, but not what we so often think. We think we are so big, when really (once you gain some perspective) we're quite small. And then we think God is so small, when really he is so big.

In the Bible, all the Songs of Scripture, like this song before us, share an important characteristic: they "make" God big. The greatness of God is their theme. I think of Mary's song in the first chapter of Luke (1:46–55). It's called the Magnificat because that's the first word

7

of her song in the Latin translation. It means (as does the original Greek), "makes large." That's what Mary's song is all about. Singing of God's strength, justice, mercy, holiness, and faithfulness, this little-in-her-own-eyes lady declares, "My soul magnifies the Lord."

That's the first song in the New Testament. The first song in the Old Testament, in Exodus 15, is little different.[3] Its theme is the magnification of God! Moses is not focused on himself, his role, or the human perspective on this event. Rather, his mind is occupied with the Lord and his mighty and unmediated acts.[4] Moses makes this hard for us to miss. The name LORD occurs ten times in this text. This is God's covenant name Yahweh, the one he gave of himself in Exodus 3, at the burning bush, revealing his eternity: "I am who I am."[5]

3. Nahum M. Sarna speaks of this song as "what may be the oldest piece of sustained poetry in the Hebrew Bible." *Exodus*, JPS Torah Commentary (New York: Jewish Publication Society, 1991), 75. Origen called it the "first song to God." R. P. Lawson, trans., *The Song of Songs: Commentary and Homilies*, ACW (New York: Paulist Press, 1957), 47. Cf. Douglas Stuart, *Exodus*, NAC (Nashville: Broadman & Holman, 2006), 346.

4. In the second half of his section on "The Poetic and Prose Accounts," Sarna describes well the God-centeredness of this song. He writes, for example, "Moses, of course, plays no active role, for it is not he who holds out his arm over the sea, as in 14:16, 21. Rather, it is the 'right hand' of God that is extended (15:12). Nor is there any mention of the angel, the cloud, and the darkness, all so prominent in 14:19–20. These intermediaries signal the distance between God and Israel; by contrast, the 'Song of the Sea' celebrates God's direct, unmediated, personal incursion into the world of humankind." Also, in his section on "Analogues," he contrasts ancient Egyptian odes with the Song, stating that the latter is distinguished by its "dominant God-centered theme." The Egyptian literature celebrates "the superhuman exploits" of the Pharaohs, but in the Torah "it is God alone who attracts the poet's interest." See *Exodus*, 75–76. Similarly, Umberto Cassuto states, "In the pagan odes of triumph, the glory of the victory is ascribed to the conquering king, but here there is not a single word of praise or glory given to Moses; these are rendered to the Lord alone." Israel Abrahams, trans., *A Commentary on the Book of Exodus* (Jerusalem: Magnes Press, 1967), 174.

5. Stuart comments, "Thus the vast majority of Israel's psalms and music about God use the name Yahweh predominantly—as a safeguard and against misuse and misunderstanding and because there is a greater sense of personal identity to the name Yahweh than to the more generic title God." *Exodus*, 348.

But Moses magnifies more than God's name, covenant, and eternity. He also magnifies God's strength: "Your right hand, O LORD, glorious in power, your right hand, O LORD, shatters the enemy" (v. 6). He also magnifies God's kingly justice and his warring wrath: "In the greatness of your majesty you overthrow your adversaries; you send out your fury; it consumes them like stubble" (v. 7).

Surprising to us, this warring wrath is one of the divine attributes Moses most magnifies. And he does so by using military metaphors. Most prominently and most strikingly is what we find in verse 3, where the LORD is called "a man of war" or (in a tamer translation) "a warrior."[6] To the enemies of God, to those who seek to strike down his people, the LORD comes with sword in hand, so to speak. The picture here is quite close to the one we find near the end of our Bibles, the picture of that mighty King of kings and Lord of lords, clothed in a robe dipped in blood, with a sword protruding from his mouth and an iron rod held firmly within his hand. He rides upon a white horse, leading the armies of heaven, and "in righteousness he judges and makes war" (see Rev. 19:11–16; cf. 1 Cor. 15:24–28).

> Dost ask who that may be? Christ Jesus, it is he;
> Lord Sabaoth his name, from age to age the same,
> And he must win the battle.[7]

6. This is what Moses predicted: that the Lord would fight for Israel (Ex. 14:14). An interesting biblical reference comes in Numbers 21:14, "the Book of the Wars of the LORD." Cf. Rabbi Judah's cross references in *Mekhilta Shirata* 4, II 30, found in *The Classic Midrash: Tannaitic Commentaries on the Bible*, translation, introduction, and commentaries by Reuven Hammer, CWS (New York: Paulist Press, 1995), 107. Cf. G. Ernest Wright, *The Old Testament and Theology* (New York: Harper & Row, 1969), 121–50. The term is likewise used in Isaiah 42:13: "The LORD goes out like a mighty man, like a man of war he stirs up his zeal; he cries out, he shouts aloud, he shows himself mighty against his foes."

7. Lord Sabaoth means "Lord of hosts" or "Lord of the armies." This comes from Luther's hymn, "A Mighty Fortress Is Our God."

This is no mild monarch. This is no wimpy warrior. This is no little God! The God here is like the one Isaiah envisioned: he is "sitting upon a throne, high and lifted up; and the train of his robe filled the temple" (Isa. 6:1). Just the train of his robe fills the whole temple! "The foundations of the thresholds" shake (6:4), the holy seraphim cover their eyes, and Isaiah says, "Woe is me! . . . for my eyes have seen the King, the LORD of hosts!" (6:5).

So Moses magnifies God's eternity, his strength, his justice, and even and especially his wrath. But he also magnifies his love or "undeserved magnanimity," as Nahum Sarna speaks of it.[8] We read this of the Lord in verse 13: "You have led in your steadfast love the people whom you have redeemed." The Lord's covenant love is patient, enduring, and merciful. He persistently loves his beloved Israel.

Two other attributes of God are addressed in the final strophe of the song, verses 13–18: sovereignty and presence, or what I'll call incarnational presence. In verse 18 we read of his kingship or sovereignty: "The LORD will reign forever and ever."[9] In verses 13 and 17, Moses speaks of God's presence on earth, likely referring prophetically to Solomon's temple as God's "place" or "abode" or "sanctuary." This reminds us again that the purpose of the exodus was worship—not merely freedom from Egyptian slavery, but freedom from Egyptian idolatry. Also, its purpose was to establish God's people under his eternal rule, in contrast to, as Sarna suggests, "the ephemeral and illusory nature of Pharaoh's self-proclaimed royal divinity."[10]

8. See Sarna, *Exodus*, 80.
9. Sarna claims this is the earliest biblical use of the metaphor of kingship in connection with the exaltation of God. Ibid., 82.
10. Ibid.

What I have found fascinating in my study of all the songs in Scripture is how this theme and these two attributes progress theologically. The two songs in Samuel continue on this note, if you will, ending by singing of God's eternal (2 Sam. 22:51) and universal (1 Sam. 2:10) reign. These themes flower in the four gospels in the person of Jesus Christ, and then culminate in the songs in the book of Revelation, which speak unapologetically of the Lord's incarnational temple-presence and his universal dominion. At the end of Scripture and history, Christ is worshipped, not merely by the nation, but by all nations (cf. Rev. 5:9). And so, with all this in mind, we can do no better than to hear with Christian ears what the Jewish scholar Umberto Cassuto says of the final verse. He summarizes Exodus 15:18 by saying, "The poem ends by proclaiming the Kingdom of Heaven."[11]

## The Prism of God's Light

Through a narrow slit in the shutters of his room at Trinity College, Cambridge, white sunlight struck the glass prism on Isaac Newton's desk, splitting into the colors of the rainbow.[12] Then and there, it dawned on him that light was a complex unity of different colors.

In 1 John 1:5, the apostle writes, "God is light." And here, through the text or "prism," if you will, of the Song of Moses, we see many of our great God's attributes: eternity, strength, justice, wrath, love, sovereignty, and incarnational presence.

The final and culminating attribute or characteristic comes in verse 11, where we learn of God's supremacy or (pick your

11. Cassuto, *Exodus*, 177.
12. I found this illustration in Alister E. McGrath, *Intellectuals Don't Need God and Other Modern Myths* (Downers Grove, IL: InterVarsity, 1993), 23.

favorite term) his "incomparability" or "total otherness" or "exclusive uniqueness."[13] This central verse is central to this God-centered song: "Who is like you, O LORD, among the gods? Who is like you, majestic in holiness, awesome in glorious deeds, doing wonders?"

Egypt's gods cannot be compared to Yahweh. Remember the plagues! What an embarrassment, comparable to the yelling and slashing prophets of Baal on Mount Carmel. Egypt's armies cannot be compared to Yahweh. The most elite forces of the world's most elite army eat dirt, the dirt at the bottom of the Red Sea.[14] Effortlessly—as easy as breathing in and out through our nose—the Lord of hosts destroys them.[15] Egypt's real rulers and awesome army cannot compare. Nor can their gods, which are "no gods" (Deut. 32:17). Nor can any unearthly beings—angels, authorities, and powers (1 Peter 3:22). Nothing and no one can compare to the Lord, our great God!

In 1952, J. B. Phillips authored an intriguing book entitled *Your God Is Too Small*. It was an apt critique of his world, and still serves as an accurate summary of ours. For many today, God is simply too small—too small in our thoughts, too small in our words, too small in our hearts. And here God's Word, through this Song of Moses, helps us, doesn't it? It helps us magnify the Lord, to "make large" our God in our souls.

13. Sarna uses the terms "incomparability" and "total otherness," while Walter C. Kaiser Jr. speaks of "exclusive uniqueness." See Sarna, *Exodus*, 76, 78, and Kaiser, "Exodus," in *Expositor's Bible Commentary*, Frank E. Gaebelein, ed., vol. 2 (Grand Rapids: Zondervan, 1990), 394.

14. On Egypt's military, see Stuart, *Exodus*, 351.

15. This idea is taken from Peter Enns, who writes, "To call the wind a nostril blast is to say that the wind is *his*. It is his to command as easily as we breathe in and out." *Exodus*, NIVAC (Grand Rapids: Zondervan, 2000), 299.

# The Evil of the Enemy

The greatness of God—that's the first plank we need to put in place if we are going to walk from the world of God's Word over into ours. The second plank is the evil of the enemy.

Two times in this text (vv. 6 and 9), God calls Pharaoh and his army "the enemy." And once they are called Israel's "adversaries" (v. 7). Now there is nothing inherently wrong with being called an enemy or an adversary. An enemy does not have to be an *evil* enemy. Jesus was an "enemy" of the scribes and Pharisees. But, here in this song, and more so in the whole story of the exodus (Ex. 1–14), we learn something of the character of Egypt's rulers and people. We learn why the adjective *evil* is appropriate.

The ancient Egyptians were one of the most amazing and advanced civilizations. This is why school children around the world still study them. I would imagine that if you have passed eighth grade you have studied something of the Pharaohs and pyramids. Those pyramids are quite amazing, aren't they? They are amazing engineering achievements. But do you know what else they are? They won't teach you this in school, but the pyramids are monuments to their monstrosity!

Who do you think built those pyramids? Do you think it was the Pharaohs and their sons—or perhaps the Egyptian middle class? No, each and every brick was laid by a slave—hundreds of thousands of slaves, decade after decade, century after century, built the pyramids. The Israelites were in bondage for "430 years" (Ex. 12:40)! Imagine all they must have built. We know from Exodus 1:11 that they built for Pharaoh two store cities, Pithom and Raamses. And we know from history that they did not build the pyramids. Those were built even before the time of Abraham.

13

But that doesn't remove the Egyptians' culpability. It only proves the point. For thousands of years, Egyptian civilization was built on the backs of broken and bloodied slaves—Israelites and others. Such oppression, and the atrocities and injustices associated with it, make the tragic experiment in American slavery seem like a blip on the radar.

## "House of Slavery"

Eleven times in Scripture, Egypt is called "the house of slavery" (Ex. 13:3, 14; 20:2; Deut. 5:6; 6:12; 7:8; 8:14; 13:5, 10; Josh. 24:17; Mic. 6:4). This nation was not merely "a house," but a "harsh" house of slavery (Ex. 6:9). The Egyptian taskmasters would beat their Hebrew slaves (Ex. 2:11). When the early chapters of Exodus speak of their slavery, the words "oppression" (3:9) and "affliction" (3:17; cf. Acts 7:34) are used.[16] Exodus 1:13–14 is a good summary of the four centuries of the Egyptians' shrewd (1:10) and sinful behavior:

> They ruthlessly made the people of Israel work as slaves and
> made their lives bitter with hard service, in mortar and brick,
> and in all kinds of work in the field. In all their work they
> ruthlessly made them work as slaves.

16. J. A. Thompson notes, "The conquest of the promised land was Yahweh's gracious activity on behalf of those who had been oppressed and outcast. But it was also an act of judgment on the people of the land. Because of their corruption the divine government decreed the end of their rule." *Deuteronomy: An Introduction and Commentary*, TOTC (Downers Grove, IL: InterVarsity, 1974), 72. Also, W. H. B. Proby says that the "bondage was not merely rigorous and cruel, as might have been the bondage of other slaves, but it was of a peculiarly uncivilizing kind." *The Ten Canticles of the Old Testament Canon: Namely the Songs of Moses (First and Second), Deborah, Hannah, Isaiah (First, Second, and Third), Hezekiah, Jonah, and Habakkuk* (London: Rivingtons, 1874), 5.

The reality of slavery—that should get to our sensibilities. Egypt was the world's largest plantation, a place where grace was as common as rain in the Desert of Paran.

Now, along with that, or more than that, the Pharaohs and the Egyptians we encounter in Exodus are often excessively violent. We certainly see this in the first chapter of Exodus, where the first Pharaoh we meet, fearing overpopulation and the growing possibly of rebellion, commands the Hebrew midwives (1:15–16), and then "all the people," to kill—to cast into the Nile River—every Hebrew baby boy (1:22). That's how, if you recall, little Moses found himself floating in that basket. The extremity of their violence resurfaces in Exodus 14 and here in 15:9. After Pharaoh (and this is the second Pharaoh) has finally agreed to let God's people go, he again (for what, the tenth time?) changes his mind. He lies to Moses and God yet again. He wants to do away with Israel. Verse 9 records his self-confident and vainglorious thoughts:[17]

> The enemy said, "I will pursue, I will overtake,
>   I will divide the spoil, my desire shall have its fill of
>     them.
>   I will draw my sword; my hand shall destroy them."

## Egyptian Idolatry

So, first, the Egyptians were cruel slave masters. Second, they were violent oppressors, even to the point of genocide—

---

17. Sarna comments on the Hebrew text: "By means of a rapid, alliterative succession of words, [the poet] mimics the arrogant self-confidence and vainglorious boasting of the foe. The omission of the conjunctions imparts to the series of verbs a staccato effect that bespeaks expectation of easy victory." *Exodus*, 79. Ryken notes that Pharaoh refers to himself six times in one verse. *Exodus*, 406.

from the slaughter of baby boys to the slaughter of all Israel. Third (and most significantly on God's scale of justice), they were idolaters.[18]

In the Bible it is stated often that God's judgment is fair. And so the wrath of God comes upon a person either for "failing to seek [God] so as to secure redemption," based on what theologians call natural revelation or what Paul calls in Romans (and I slightly paraphrase) "what is obvious to all through creation,"[19] or for spurning God, directly rejecting what he has graciously revealed about himself, whether it is the full gospel in the revelation of our Lord Jesus Christ, or (as we have here) what Pharaoh learned and knew of God.

In Exodus 5:1, Moses and Aaron go to Pharaoh and say, "Thus says the LORD, the God of Israel, 'Let my people go, that they may hold a feast to me in the wilderness.'" Now Pharaoh's response at this point is fairly innocent: "But Pharaoh said, 'Who is the LORD, that I should obey his voice and let Israel go? I do not know the LORD'" (v. 2). I don't know the Lord. He has no authority over me. So I'm not letting you all go. That's his initial thought.

That's chapter 5. But as we get through chapters 6, 7, 8, 9, 10, 11, and 12, you better believe Pharaoh gets to know the Lord. Ten plagues later, he knows very well who the Lord is, more

18. For a classic poem on this same theme, see George Gordon Bryon (Lord Byron), "The Destruction of Sennacherib," in *War Poems*, ed. John Hollander, Everyman's Library Pocket Poets (New York: Knopf, 1999), 21–22. The final line is this:

And the widows of Ashur are loud in their wail,
And the idols are broke in the temple of Baal;
And the might of the Gentile, unsmote by the sword,
Hath melted like snow in the glance of the Lord!

19. Robert W. Yarbrough, "Jesus on Hell," in *Hell Under Fire: Modern Scholarship Reinvents Eternal Punishment*, ed. Christopher W. Morgan and Robert A. Peterson (Grand Rapids: Zondervan, 2004), 68.

so than most men in history. This phrase is repeated in these chapters: "in the sight of Pharaoh" (5:21; 7:20; 9:8; cf. 11:3). All that God did in Egypt happened in the sight of Pharaoh, right before his very eyes.

In this way, Pharaoh functions as a Judas-like figure. Judas witnessed with his own eyes the work of God in the incarnation, and yet he rejected that revelation. Similarly, Pharaoh witnessed the power of God over all of nature and over all of the Egyptian gods he believed in, and yet, as we hear over and over, "Pharaoh hardened his heart" (7:13–14, 22, 23; 8:15, 19, 32; 9:7, 34–35). After witnessing all the wonders of God (11:10)—can you imagine witnessing such miracles?—he remained faithful to his false religion, trusting in the magic of his magicians and viewing himself, either in this life or the next, to be divine. What audacity! What arrogance! What idolatry.

## An Evil Empire

During the heat of the Cold War, President Reagan called the Soviet Union, for all their atrocities, an "evil empire." I don't want to rank evil empires, but the Egyptians are up there. Like the Canaanites, the Assyrians, the Babylonians, and the Romans in Bible times, and many other nations in modern times, they were no saintly society (see Deut. 9:4–5). And so their centuries of oppression and affliction (cf. Gen. 15:13) and murder and idolatry and pride deserved punishment, deserved the heavy weight of the waves of God's wrath.

So can you start to see why Moses and Miriam and the men, women, and children of Israel could burst into song and start to dance—why they could sing "his praise" when "the waters covered their adversaries"?[20] Think of it this way: if you were held hostage for only ten days, each day having to work in a sweat shop, and one day the U.S. Army Special Forces crashed through the back door, killed the enemy, and rescued you, wouldn't you sing of your salvation and dance for joy? Wouldn't you rejoice in just judgment? I bet you would.

⁻ You see, I don't actually think we are so far removed from what we read here. We simply have this thin layer of unscriptural insensitivity over our eyes; if it were surgically removed by the scalpel of God's Spirit, we would see things as they truly are. We would understand that there is a time for everything under heaven—a time to be gracious, a time to forgive, a time to love our enemies, but also a time to rejoice when evil is eradicated.[21]

A few years ago, I kept track of all the one-line CNN stories on my Google homepage for one month. What I noticed was intriguing. Nearly half of the headlines were designed to tap into the nerve of normal human moral conscience, to get us outraged by injustice. Just look at a few. I think you'll get a feel for what I'm saying:

Explosion kills 41 in Afghanistan
Babies get blood thinner overdose in hospital
Bodies of 2 U.S. soldiers found in Iraq

20. "And the waters covered their adversaries; not one of them was left. Then they believed his words; they sang his praise" (Ps. 106:11–12).

21. I like how Stuart puts the same sentiment. Commenting on verse 7, he writes, "An important theological truth is incorporated here, namely that God's eventual destruction of those who opposed him and his anger against evil are not opposed to God's majesty but are in fact inherent aspects of it. Modern sentimentalist thinking wants God to be ever-tolerant, always softhearted, and thus defines God's justice as something other than how the Bible defines it. . . . Those offended by these facts about God are wishing for a reality that has never existed. He does get mad; he does smash his foes, and he is majestic in doing so." *Exodus*, 352.

North Korea blames South Korea for tourist shooting
Sudan's president charged with genocide
Girl, 10, says husband raped, abused her
Pope says sorry for "evil" of clergy sex abuse
Child molester stays out of prison
Police: Preacher killed wife, put her in freezer

Now, Google or CNN doesn't say it any more than the ten o'clock news does. They don't say, "Well, isn't this wrong? Isn't this stuff evil?" They know that such headlines will be of human interest because human beings long for justice in an unjust world. Humans hate inhumanity. And Christians, who are made in the image of God, but are also remade into the image of Christ, like the God we serve, ought to *hate* inhumanity and cruelty and wickedness and arrogance and idolatry. C. S. Lewis once said, "The Jews cursed their enemies bitterly because they took right and wrong seriously."[22] Now, that's right, isn't it? You better believe that's right.

The evil of the enemy: that's our second plank.


## The Substance of Salvation

So, do you see how we are building this bridge? First we have the good character of God, and second the bad character of the Egyptians. These two concepts can help us get our modern, squeamish, unmanly minds around what is before us in

22. Lewis is quoted in William Sanford LaSor et al., *Old Testament Survey: The Message, Form, and Background of the Old Testament* (Grand Rapids: Eerdmans, 1996), 321. And Lewis had what I would deem a less than orthodox view of the imprecatory psalms. See his chapter on "The Cursings" in *Reflections on the Psalms* (New York: Harcourt, Brace, and Company, 1958), 20–33.

the Song of Moses. These two planks help us walk from their world to ours.

Now, our third and final plank—*the substance of salvation*—takes us all the way across.

## Saved from What?

"Are you saved?" If I were to ask you that question, what would you say? If I were to ask most evangelicals across this country, what would they say? Well, they would say, as you would likely say, "Oh yes, I'm saved." But what if I asked this follow-up question: "Saved from what?" I might hear such answers as these:

I'm saved from loneliness.
I'm saved from poverty.
I'm saved from a bad marriage.
I'm saved from an addiction.
I'm saved from a life without purpose.
I'm saved from my worst life now.

And then someone will say (and thankfully so), "I'm saved from my sin." But who these days will ever say, "I'm saved from the wrath of God"—the waters or the fire of God's holy judgment?

Just listen to Christian testimonies. How many of them sound like Scripture? How many of them sound like Christians of old? How many people think and talk about what they were saved from—sin or the devil or fiery judgment?[23]

23. The Hebrew in Exodus 15:12, along with other biblical texts, may refer to "the underworld," as Sarna notes (*Exodus*, 80)—or even "hell," as Stuart says (*Exodus*, 355). Moreover, Stuart points out how the metaphor for "swallowing" in verse 7 "reflects

But Paul once wrote to the Thessalonians about how they responded to the gospel, saying of them, "You turned to God from idols to serve the living and true God, and to wait for his Son from heaven, whom he raised from the dead, Jesus who delivers us from the wrath to come" (1 Thess. 1:9–10). Jesus delivers us. He saves us. He saves us from something. He saves us from the wrath to come!

Let's think about the three most prominent images of salvation provided for us in the first two books of the Bible, Genesis and Exodus. See if you see a pattern. First we have the great flood. God sees the world is totally wicked. Noah preaches for a long time (oh, the patience of God!), "Repent, come into the ark, find refuge from the coming storm." But no one listens, so only eight are saved. Saved from what? They are saved from the judgment of God, the 960 hours of the rain of God's wrath. That's the first image.

The second image is the Passover, the final plague. Do you remember it as a plague? It was! Take a lamb, God tells his people—a perfect, spotless lamb. Sacrifice it and brush its blood upon the doorpost of your house. Why? It will be a sign that you believe, but also a protection from the angel of death, who will pass through Egypt judging disbelief and disobedience. And so, the wrath of God comes to town and passes over those who trust and obey God's word.

The final image is what we have here in Exodus 14 and 15—the parting and closing of the Red Sea. The Egyptian soldiers are about to catch up to the Israelites. The people lament their impending doom, "O great, we're going to die!" But God says, "Trust me. Moses, strike the water with your rod." What happens? The waters part, and the Israelites walk safely from one side to the

---

the common theme of divine judgment by fire" (p. 353). He cites ten biblical texts, including Leviticus 21:9.

other. But that doesn't save the Israelites! No, the Egyptians start to do the same. They start through the Red Sea, down the same parted path. What then saves the Israelites? They are saved when the waters come back and drown the Egyptians.

Are you saved? Saved from what? If you believe in Jesus Christ as your ark of refuge, as your spotless lamb, as the only "way" from this side to that side, then you will be saved from the storm, and from death, and from the waves of the fire of God's wrath on the last day. This is what the first two books of the Bible teach us, as does the last.

## The Song of Moses and the Triumph of the Lamb

As mentioned earlier, the book of Revelation contains a number of songs, all of them important to our study. After we leave the throne room and the angelic chorus singing "Holy, holy, holy, is the Lord God Almighty, who was and is and is to come!" (4:8), we hear the Song of the Lamb, where Jesus is praised as God, for he alone has been found worthy to open the scroll and break its seven seals: "Worthy are you . . . for . . . by your blood you ransomed people for God from every tribe and language and people and nation" (5:9). Now, what is Jesus alone worthy to do? He alone is worthy to open the seals. And what are these seals? Well, they represent the coming wrath of God. When the wrath comes, the kings of the earth will hide themselves in caves and call out to the mountains and the rocks, "Fall on us and hide us from the face of him who is seated on the throne, and from the wrath of the Lamb, for the great day of their wrath has come, and who can stand?" (6:16–17).

Now, this theme of wrath is not going to disappear. No, in the rest of Revelation it grows and spreads like a California wildfire on a windy day. So, when we get to Revelation 15, look at what John sees:

> Then I saw another sign in heaven, great and amazing, seven angels with seven plagues, which are the last, for with them the wrath of God is finished. And I saw what appeared to be a sea of glass mingled with fire—and also those who had conquered the beast and its image and the number of its name, standing beside the sea of glass with harps of God in their hands. And they sing *the song of Moses*,[24] the servant of God, and the song of the Lamb, saying,

> "Great and amazing are your deeds,
>   O Lord God the Almighty!
> Just and true are your ways,
>   O King of the nations!
> Who will not fear, O Lord,
>   and glorify your name?
> For you alone are holy.
>   All nations will come
>   and worship you,
> for your righteous acts have been revealed." (15:1–4)

24. Michael Tilly takes "the song of Moses" here to be a reference to Deuteronomy (due mostly to similarities of language in Revelation 15:3–5). See "Deuteronomy in Revelation," in *Deuteronomy in the New Testament*, ed. Maarten J. J. Menken and Steve Moyise (New York: T&T Clark, 2007), 154. But I agree with G. K. Beale that the song in Revelation 15 refers primarily to Exodus 15, but also includes Deuteronomy 32 (as it fits in with the theme in Revelation of "judgment on apostate Christians"). See *The Book of Revelation: A Commentary on the Greek Text*, NIGTC (Grand Rapids: Eerdmans, 1999), 791–95, 783. Note also that this is proof that the Song of Moses was known by the early church. For other evidence that this song was sung throughout Israel's history, see Pss. 118:14; 136:13; 140:7.

You see, the New Testament doesn't envision salvation any differently than the Old Testament.[25] We just have more of the facts and key players in place. The earthly victory has become a cosmic one; "Egypt" has become "the ends of the earth."[26] The same story, the identical image, is here. There is evil in the world. God sees it. God is going to do something about it. Flee from the wrath to come. Flee into the arms of the coming judge, the only one who stretched out his hands in love for us, dying in our place, taking on our sin, our judgment, our hell. "Hallelujah! Salvation and glory and power belong to our God" (Rev. 19:1).[27]

## Attune Our Voices

If you split certain atoms (and don't do this at home), what happens? Kaboom! Likewise, if one splits or tears asunder what God has joined together—the love of God from the wrath of God, the mercy of God from the justice of God—the gospel, the good news, explodes! Or take water, this necessary, life-giving substance ($H_2O$). If you remove but one atom of hydrogen from a molecule of water, what do you get? You get hydroxide, which, when combined with various other molecules, produces (if consumed in the right quantities) a deadly substance.

25. While I disagree with much of his exegesis and theology, I fully agree with the first sentence of George A. F. Knight's postscript: "No line can be drawn to separate the theology of the Song of Moses and the theology of the NT, summed up as it is in what Rev. 15:3 calls the Song of the Lamb." *The Song of Moses: A Theological Quarry* (Grand Rapids: Eerdmans, 1995), 139.

26. See Terence E. Fretheim, *Exodus*, Interpretation (Louisville: Westminster John Knox, 1991).

27. Sarna notes how in Exodus 15:2 the "Hebrew *yah* is an abbreviation of the divine name YHVH" and how this poetic form "has survived in English in 'hallelujah.'" *Exodus*, 77.

Today there is something deadly, subtly deadly, in our preaching of the "gospel." We have either completely removed wrath from the substance of it, or we have simply taken a bit of wrath away, enough to make people "like" God and "like" Jesus, and "like" our church and "like" us—but also just enough to kill them, by not giving them, as our Lord put it, "a spring of *water* welling up to eternal life" (John 4:14).

I believe it was G. K. Chesterton who once wrote, "The danger when men stop believing in God is not that they'll believe in nothing, but that they'll believe in anything." We live in a world where people believe in anything and everything except that which is really real—in reincarnation but not resurrection, in horoscopes but not hell, in luck but not the Lord. We also live in a time when the church thinks so much like the world—not that we believe in reincarnation over against resurrection, but that we believe in God's love over against his wrath. This is why the Song of Moses matters, and why it is a song to which we must attune our voices—singing of the greatness of God, singing for joy over the destruction of evil, and singing in thanksgiving for the full salvation we have in Christ.

3 aspects of this song
1) The greatness of God
2) The joy over destrctn of evil
3) thanksgvg for full salvation fr. God's wrath, thru Jesus

Give ear, O heavens, and I will speak,
  and let the earth hear the words of my mouth.
[2] May my teaching drop as the rain,
  my speech distill as the dew,
like gentle rain upon the tender grass,
  and like showers upon the herb.
[3] For I will proclaim the name of the LORD;
  ascribe greatness to our God!
[4] The Rock, his work is perfect,
  for all his ways are justice.
A God of faithfulness and without iniquity,
  just and upright is he.
. . . . . . . . . . . . . . . . . . . .

[43] Rejoice with him, O heavens;
  bow down to him, all gods,
for he avenges the blood of his children
  and takes vengeance on his adversaries.
He repays those who hate him
  and cleanses his people's land. (Deut. 32:1–4, 43)

# 2

# The Song of Yahweh: An Exodus from Israel's Apostasy

⟨⟨⟨⟩⟩⟩

A MAN'S LAST WORDS often summarize what was first in his heart.[1] The influential nineteenth-century clergyman Henry Ward Beecher, brother of Harriet Beecher Stowe, became a national figure for his sensational adultery trial, his acceptance of Darwinism, and his rejection of the divinity of Jesus. His final words expressed well his growing religious skepticism. Before he

---

1. Especially interesting to this study is Steven Weitzman's chapter on Deuteronomy 32, entitled "Swan Song," which begins in this way: "In the collective imagination of the ancient world the most significant words of a person's lifetime were those spoken just before death. . . . This fascination with the words of dying is reflected in dozens of texts from the ancient Near East and Mediterranean which purport to be the final speeches or testaments of kings, sages, and other figure of high social status." *Song and Story in Biblical Narrative: The History of a Literary Convention in Ancient Israel* (Bloomington, IN: Indiana University Press, 1997), 37.

breathed his last breath, he said, "Now comes the mystery." The last words of Wilhelm Hegel, the German philosopher whose writings are notorious for their obscurity, highlighted both his arrogance and his incomprehensibility when he said, "Only one man ever understood me. And he really didn't understand me." Voltaire, the French Enlightenment thinker, had no love for Christ and Christianity. Of Christ he said, "Curse the wretch!" He boasted, "In twenty years Christianity will be no more. My single hand shall destroy the edifice it took twelve apostles to rear." He was wrong about both. Shortly after his death, his house became the depot for the Geneva Bible Society, and today Christianity is the largest religion in the world. It is reported that when Voltaire was asked on his deathbed to renounce Satan, he jested, "This is no time to make new enemies." Another source speaks of his physician testifying this to be Voltaire's deathbed cry: "I am abandoned by God and man! I will give you half of what I am worth if you will give me six months' life. Then I shall go to hell and you will go with me."[2] Either scenario speaks loudly of his hard heart.

The economist Karl Marx, the controversial figure responsible for the theory of communism, was asked by his housekeeper shortly before he died if he had any final words. To this he replied (perhaps reflective of his atheism and certainly of his anger), "Go on, get out! Last words are for fools who haven't said enough!"

In Deuteronomy 32–33, we have the last words of Moses. In chapter 33, we have his blessing on Israel, in chapter 32 his song. And here, in this second (cf. Ex. 15) but last song, we find that Moses' last words reflect his life of faith (see Heb. 11:24–29), his trust in God, and his obedience to God's word, despite what

2. For the second scenario, see R. Kent Hughes, *Hebrews*, PTW (Wheaton, IL: Crossway, 1993), 2:41–42.

he knows is about to happen.[3] He knows that he (Deut. 31:2), due to a moment of mistrust (he "broke faith"—see Numbers 12:14; 20:1–13),[4] will be buried across from the Promised Land in a place where his people will soon forget (Deut. 34:6).[5] He will die without obtaining that promise. And he knows that God's people, after Joshua's good generation, will be no better than Moses' generation, who perished in the wilderness (Deut. 1:26–27, 35; cf. Judg. 2:10). He may even know that Joshua's generation would be the last fully faithful generation until the time of God's ultimate prophet, priest, and king.

He knows all this, and yet he dies a prophet's death, with the very words of God on his mouth. And I say "the very words of God" because God calls Moses into the Tent of Meeting (31:14) and then commands him (31:19) to write "this song," this God-inspired, God-dictated, God-filled song.[6] Moses is

3. If one were Moses, it would be tempting to heed the counsel of Job's wife, "to curse God and die," or to mirror the exodus generation, with their grumblings and stubbornness and rebellion (e.g., Deut. 31:27). But this man, who alone has seen God (his backside), here sees God eye to eye.

4. For a short but helpful summary of the "reason for Moses' exclusion," see J. G. McConville, *Deuteronomy*, AOTC (Downers Grove, IL: InterVarsity, 2002), 460.

5. This perhaps was the case to show Israel and us that Moses wasn't the perfect prophet, and that we should look to one better than Moses (see Heb. 1). Theodoret of Cyrus asks, "Why was it that, for such a slight fault, Moses was commanded to view the land from afar and forbidden to lead in the people?" The early church commentator gives two reasons. The first has to do with God's higher standards for more "perfected" people. Although God shows, in Theodoret's own words, "long-suffering to others who are guilty of grave transgressions, he does not make such an allowance for the saints." God's second reason was "to prevent the Israelites from worshiping him as God." See Robert C. Hill, trans., *The Questions on the Octateuch*, LEC (Washington, DC: Catholic University of America Press, 2007), 2:246–47.

6. Daniel Block, in a draft of his forthcoming commentary on Deuteronomy, suggests this song should be called "the Song of Yahweh," not only because it was "directly inspired" by him and because "a major portion of the Song is cast in the first person as divine speech (vv. 21–35; 39–42)," but also because it was "apparently dictated by him to Joshua and Moses in the Tent of Meeting (31:14–15)." See

to "write this song" and then "teach it to the people"—to "put it in their mouths" (v. 19).

## A Witness and a Warning

But why? Why write it? Why teach it? Why teach it so everyone would know it by heart, being able to sing it on the streets or in the synagogue?

It is to be taught, memorized, and sung because this song will serve as a national anthem of sorts,[7] one which reminds them not of their great history as a nation, but of their great apostasy.[8] As God's people are poised to enter the Promised Land, over the Jordan River, this song is to serve as a "witness" (31:19) against them. This will be no song celebrating their freedom in the Lord and their exodus from the bondage of Egypt, but rather one that bemoans their incessant slavery to idolatry. It will be a witness against them, like a witness in a murder trial who points the finger at the accused and says, "Yes! That's the man I saw. He did it. He's guilty."[9]

It will serve as a witness, but also as a "warning" (32:46),[10] a gracious warning for all the generations to come, even ours. This is what we find in 32:44–47 (cf. 31:30). There we read,

Deuteronomy, NIVAC (Grand Rapids: Zondervan, forthcoming), 1109 (in the draft edition I used).

7. Block calls this chapter "Israel's national anthem" in Deuteronomy.

8. John Calvin says it well: "Doubtless he would have desired to leave a pleasing and joyful recollection of himself, and therefore would willingly have exhorted them to the performance of their duties, either with blandness, or at any rate with placidity, but their stubbornness compelled him to testify his indignation in the severity of his address." Charles William Bingham, trans., Commentaries on the Four Last Books of Moses (repr., Grand Rapids: Baker, 1979), 334.

9. Another scriptural song that is against God's people is the song in Isaiah 5, which bemoans Israel's injustices.

10. I like how Nicetas of Remesiana, in his work Liturgical Singing, states it: "Moses again, when about to depart from this life, sang a fear-inspiring canticle in

Moses came and recited all the words of this song in the hearing of the people, he and Joshua the son of Nun. And when Moses had finished speaking all these words to all Israel, he said to them, "Take to heart all the words by which I am *warning* you today, that you may command them to your children, that they may be careful to do all the words of this law. For it is no empty word for you, but your very life, and by this word you shall live long in the land that you are going over the Jordan to possess."

We have two songs of Moses in the Bible. The first song, in Exodus 15, is a *war song*, addressing Egypt's evil and God's victory over it. The second song, here in Deuteronomy 32, is a *warning song*, addressing Israel's evil and God's victory over it.

How interesting—yet how odd! For when is the last time you came to church and sang a song of war or a song of warning? We often sing about the greatness, justice, perfection, purity, and faithfulness of God, as Moses does in verses 2–3; and of God's undeserved mercy and atonement for sin, as in verses 36 and 43; and sometimes (maybe once or twice a decade!) of God's wrath on rebellion, his vengeance against vices, his execution of idolaters, as Moses does throughout much of this song. But when do we ever sing words of warning? When do we ever "teach and *admonish* one another," as Paul tells us to in Colossians 3:16, by "singing psalms and hymns and spiritual songs," spiritual songs like this one? I don't know if we ever do.

And I'm not sure, given this scriptural command and common sense, why this is the case; for I can't think of a warning in

---

Deuteronomy. He left the songs as a sort of testament to the people of Israel, to teach them the kind of funeral they should expect, if ever they abandoned God." See Joseph T. Lienhard, ed., *Exodus, Leviticus, Numbers, Deuteronomy*, ACCS (Downers Grove, IL: InterVarsity, 2001), 331.

this world that is not gracious and is not motivated by love or at least some concern. For example:

> Don't touch. That's hot. You'll burn yourself.
> Slow down, dangerous curve. You'll run off the road.
> Poison: do not drink or you'll die.
> Let him who thinks he stands take heed lest he fall.[11]

Warnings are good. They are gracious calls which seek to protect us from danger or harm. And this is precisely what is before us here. Moses writes a song of warning, a loving song of warning, one that he hopes will fall "like gentle rain upon the tender grass" (v. 2), seeping deep down into their hard hearts (v. 46) and ours, so that we might grow to fear, love, obey, and serve God in this generation.

## Remember the Days of Old

This song has two major warnings. The first is a warning against forgetfulness. Earlier in Deuteronomy, Moses tells his privileged generation to "take care . . . lest you *forget* the things that your eyes have seen, and lest they depart from your heart all the days of your life" (4:9). Similar admonitions are given throughout this book and throughout this song, most notably in verse 7, which begins, "Remember the days of old."[12]

11. Cf. 1 Corinthians 10:13. First Corinthians contains a few allusions to the Song of Moses. E.g., compare "Shall we provoke the Lord?" (1 Cor. 10:22) and "They have provoked me" (Deut. 32:21 LXX). See Brian S. Rosner, "Deuteronomy in 1 and 2 Corinthians," in *Deuteronomy in the New Testament*, ed. Maarten J. J. Menken and Steve Moyise (New York: T&T Clark, 2007), 130–32.

12. Block calls verses 5–18 "The Recollection" and verses 7–14 "A Call to Remember Yahweh's Grace." *Deuteronomy*, 1:122.

The word "remember" is important in the Bible.[13] It's used sixteen times in Deuteronomy,[14] and hundreds of times throughout Scripture. We think of the Passover or the Feast of Unleavened Bread, which was instituted, as Exodus 12:14 records, as "a memorial day." To remember the exodus from Egypt, God's people were to celebrate this feast annually. Similarly, in our Christian context, during the Lord's Supper we remember Jesus' death, which saves us from bondage to sin. "Do this," Jesus said, "in remembrance of me" (Luke 22:19). This need for Christians to remember is also Peter's explicit purpose in writing his two epistles:

> This is now the second letter that I am writing to you, beloved. In both of them I am stirring up your sincere mind *by way of reminder*, that you should *remember* the predictions of the holy prophets and the commandment of the Lord and Savior through your apostles. (2 Peter 3:1–2)

Peter calls them to remember the words of God. As we remember the words and works of God, we are to remember the person of God. This concept is important in the Bible and to biblical faith.

Now, why is the concept of remembrance so important? It's important because forgetfulness is not neutral. To not remember is to replace; to not remember God is to replace him with other gods, which are no gods at all (cf. Isa. 17:10). This is spelled

13. Walter Brueggemann notes, "Israel's primal utterance in worship is *an act of remembrance*." *Worship in Ancient Israel: An Essential Guide* (Nashville: Abingdon, 2005), 39.

14. J. A. Thompson notes, "The verb *zakar*, 'remember,' occurs no less than sixteen times in Deuteronomy with particular reference to the deliverance from Egypt (7:18; 8:2, 14; 9:7; 16:12; 24:9, *etc.*)." *Deuteronomy: An Introduction and Commentary*, TOTC (Downers Grove, IL: InterVarsity, 1974), 77.

out with great clarity in Romans 1:18–25, where Paul talks about taking the glory due to God alone and giving it to idols, worshipping the creation instead of the Creator. And in our text we find the same thought.

After the greatness of God's person and works are exalted and explained (vv. 3–14),[15] we learn that Israel has forsaken the living God to worship dead idols (vv. 15–18). Such apostasy through idolatry is what provokes God to anger and invites future judgment (vv. 19–33). Although the Lord is their father (v. 6, and often in this song), he will disown his children, those who refuse to remember. Ironically, he will disown those, as verse 7 puts it (cf. v. 17), who forget to ask their earthly fathers about their heavenly one. Verse 18 records the indictment against Israel: "You were *unmindful* of the Rock that bore you, and you *forgot* the God who gave you birth."

Do you see the tragic picture here? While the Lord has been faithful—strong, sure, and secure like a "rock"—his people have chosen to build upon the sand (cf. Matt. 7:26). And although God has been like a mother and a father, bringing them to life (choosing to be merciful to them out of all the nations), they have forgotten such kindness.


## The Novelty of Idolatry

Why would they do this? Why did they not remember to remember? This song gives us two reasons for their forgetfulness and their subsequent idolatry. (And you might be surprised to see how relevant these are to us.) The big picture, given to

15. It is interesting to note that compared with many psalms and all the other songs of Scripture, the details of God's works here are more blurred or generalized. McConville calls this a "generalized memory." *Deuteronomy*, 461.

us throughout the Old Testament, is that the people of Israel apostatize because they want to be acceptable to their surrounding culture. In the specific context of this song, they want the Canaanites to like them.

That major reason, you might say, is under the surface, like the rot that leads to a root canal. But Moses sings about two reasons. First, they desired to try something new. Verse 17 touches on this point. "They sacrificed to demons that were no gods, to gods they had never known, to new gods that had come recently." Novelty! "Why would I worship the God of my fathers? That's old. That's boring. I want something new and exciting: the latest god, the newest religious trend." That was their attitude, and so often ours.

Why is it that I can go to the religion section of a bookstore and find signs above six full bookcases that read, "New Age"?[16] And why can I find next to the bookcase for "Bibles" the sign, "Eastern Religions"? Why are so many Americans interested in Buddhism or Islam or scientology or astrology or paganism or witchcraft or voodoo or cults or animal worship or you name it? There are a number of reasons, but I think the top one is novelty! If Harry Potter started a religion, many people who don't go to church would join it, just for the novelty of it.

Today if you ask someone who is into the newest thing, let's say Buddhism, or Buddhism mixed with a pinch of New Age and a touch of mystical Catholicism (that's a popular one where I live), "So, do you think what you believe is truer than Christianity?" his or her reply wouldn't be, "Oh yes," but, "Who cares? It works for me." And, best of all, it's "new." That means

---

16. What is called "new" in the New Age movement is simply old paganism, close to the cult of the Canaanites. The devil simply recycles what has worked, putting new dust jackets on old books.

exciting or improved.[17] G. K. Chesterton once said, "The Christian ideal has not been tried and found wanting. It has been found difficult; and left untried."[18] But these days I'm not even sure if it's been found difficult at all. People today don't know if Christianity is good or bad, old or new, boring or exciting, true or false, hard or easy.

Israel forgot God for the latest religious fad—what was cool in their new Canaanite culture. We must be careful that we don't do the same.

Second, Israel was forgetful because they grew fat. Now, this is the big one (pun intended)! In our text, this is the main cause of their idolatry. Earlier in Deuteronomy, God's people were warned about what might happen in the all-you-can-eat Promised Land: "When you eat and are full, then take care lest you forget the LORD" (6:11–12; cf. 8:11–14). Now, the feasting is not the problem. Food is a bountiful blessing from God. Heaven will be a wedding banquet, Jesus' first miracle times a thousand. God is saving the best wine for last. The problem is not the food or the drink, but the forgetting which a full stomach can cause (cf. Prov. 30:8–9).

In verses 11–13 of our text, Moses speaks of God's gracious provision, providing produce and honey and oil even in the

17. I agree with Ralph Waldo Emerson's famous saying in his essay, "Self-Reliance": "A foolish consistency is the hobgoblin of little minds." *Self-reliance and Other Essays* (repr., New York: Dover, 1993), 24. There is wise consistency and foolish consistency. Israel's is foolish. Israel has, as Calvin states, a "perverse love of novelty." *Commentaries on the Four Last Books of Moses*, 351. There is a wonderful example of this perverse love of novelty in C. S. Lewis, *The Screwtape Letters* (New York: Macmillan, 1948). There the archdevil, Screwtape, counsels Wormwood, his understudy, "The horror of the Same Old Thing is one of the most valuable passions we have produced in the human heart—an endless source of heresies in religion" (p. 126).

18. Gilbert K. Chesterton, *What's Wrong with the World* (New York: Dodd, Mead and Company, 1912), 48.

barren desert of Sinai (cf. 2:7). Then in verse 14, his thought focuses either on the fertile and lush lands of the Transjordan,[19] where this song was likely composed, or across the Jordan River in the Promised Land itself, thus speaking prophetically about all that that land will offer. Either way, all the food and drink described in verse 14 has made God's people forgetfully fat: "But Jeshurun[20] grew fat, and kicked; you grew fat, stout, and sleek; then he forsook God who made him and scoffed at the Rock of his salvation" (v. 15). Note the progression:

> They grew fat,
>> then they forsook God,
>>> and then they even scoffed at their Savior!

Israel was to live, as said earlier in Deuteronomy and later by our Lord Jesus, not "by bread alone," but "by every word that comes from the mouth of the LORD" (Deut. 8:3; cf. Matt. 4:4). Yet what do we find here? We find that they are looking down at the ground, gorging themselves like brute beasts, ignoring the hand that feeds them, until finally, when they come up for a breath of air, they look up and scoff, "Who are you? Give me more." Their god had become their belly, as Paul puts it in Philippians 3:19. They were so full of food (which made them so fat of body and so fat of mind), that there was simply no room for God.

This is a real spiritual problem in our world, isn't it? Why is it that those who are most hungry are so often most hungry for the Word and hungry for God? Have you ever thought about that?

19. See Eugene H. Merrill, *Deuteronomy*, NAC (Nashville: Broadman & Holman, 1994), 415.
20. Jeshurun is a "pet name" that God sometimes used for Israel. It literally means "the upright one," used here ironically or sarcastically. See Peter C. Craigie, *The Book of Deuteronomy*, NICOT (Grand Rapids: Eerdmans, 1976), 382.

And why is the opposite true? And why is it that our Lord Jesus never offered warnings about the spiritual dangers of poverty or hunger? Instead, we find teaching after teaching about the possible spiritual disadvantages of wealth and abundance.

Think of the story Jesus told of the rich man and Lazarus, the first going to hell and the latter to heaven. Lazarus may have lived off crumbs, but he lived for the world to come. The rich man, however, "feasted sumptuously every day" (Luke 16:19). His face was so full he made no room for Moses and the Prophets, no effort to digest God's words of wisdom and warning into his soul. Or think of the rich young ruler, who, due to his abundance of possessions and his unwillingness to forgo them to follow Jesus, was, to our Lord, like a fat camel who couldn't push his way through the eye of the needle into the kingdom of God (Mark 10:17–25). Or think of the parable of the sower, about the seed which fell among the thorns. Do you remember what happened? The seed of the word of the gospel was choked by "the cares of the world and the deceitfulness of riches and the desires for other things" (Mark 4:19). Or think of our Lord's words of warning and rebuke to the church of Laodicea. In Revelation 3:15–16, we learn of their lukewarm faith, and then in verse 17 we discover that this is tied to their material fatness. They say to themselves and of themselves, "I am rich, I have prospered, and I need nothing." But Jesus calls them poor, blind, and naked. Or, finally, think of the Sermon on the Plain, in which Jesus says quite plainly,

> Blessed are you who are poor, for yours is the kingdom of God. Blessed are you who are hungry now, for you shall be satisfied. . . . But woe to you who are rich, for you have received your consolation. Woe to you who are full now, for you shall be hungry. (Luke 6:20–21, 24–25)

38

It might do us well, even now, to ask the question Jesus asked a long time ago: "For what will it profit a man if he gains the whole world and forfeits his life?" (Matt. 16:26). The people of Israel lost their soul because their fatness made them turn *from* God—and turn *on* God. How could they sing and dance in praise of God's victory, as we saw in the *Te Deum* of Triumph, and then curse and trample on God's good name, as we have here? Here's how: they didn't watch their weight! They grew too fat.

## Be Careful to Obey

Here in the second Song of Moses, Moses sings a song of warning. And the first major warning is *to remember*. Be careful, Moses says, not to forget God, for forgetting will lead to idolatry and idolatry to divine judgment. Now, the second warning is *to be careful to obey the law so as to live long in the land*.

Again we turn to verses 46–47 as our hermeneutical key in unlocking this text. There Moses says:

> Take to heart all the words by which I am *warning* you today, that you may command them to your children, that they may *be careful to do all the words of this law*. For it is no empty word for you, but your very life, and by this word you shall live long in the land that you are going over the Jordan to possess.

Now, when we see language like "be careful to do all the words of this law," we might mistakenly think that God is calling them to obey the law so he might love them. But that is never, according to Scripture, the way God works. Think of the giving of the Ten Commandments. How does Exodus 20 begin? It begins with grace, with God's act of salvation in the past: "I am the Lord your God, who brought you out of the land of Egypt" (v. 2). God's love comes before his law. And God's law is a law of love. How does our Lord Jesus summarize it? "Love the Lord your God . . . love your neighbor" (Mark 12:29–31). William Tyndale, the sixteenth-century Reformer and Bible translator, reiterated this point well when he wrote this about Deuteronomy:

> [It is] a book worthy to be read in, day and night, and never to be out of hands: for it is the most excellent of all the books of Moses. It is . . . a preaching of faith and love . . . to love God out of faith, and the love of a man's neighbor out of the love of God.[21]

So we are to see the warning in verse 46—"Be careful to do all the words of this law"— in the context of the whole of Scripture, but also in the context of this song, at the end of which we read of God's unending mercy. Here we have, as J. A. Thompson nicely puts it, "a soliloquy in the heart of God."[22] Run your eyes through verses 36–43:

> For the Lord will vindicate his people
>     and have compassion on his servants,
> when he sees that their power is gone
>     and there is none remaining, bond or free.
> Then he will say, "Where are their gods,
>     the rock in which they took refuge,
> who ate the fat of their sacrifices
>     and drank the wine of their drink offering?
> Let them rise up and help you;

21. Cited in Raymond Brown, *The Message of Deuteronomy*, BST (Downers Grove, IL: InterVarsity, 1993), 27.
22. Thompson, *Deuteronomy*, 301 (on verses 26–38).

let them be your protection!
See now that I, even I, am he,
    and there is no god beside me;
I kill and I make alive;
    I wound and I heal;
    and there is none that can deliver out of my hand.
For I lift up my hand to heaven
    and swear, As I live forever,
if I sharpen my flashing sword
    and my hand takes hold on judgment,
I will take vengeance on my adversaries
    and will repay those who hate me.
I will make my arrows drunk with blood,
    and my sword shall devour flesh—
with the blood of the slain and the captives,
    from the long-haired heads of the enemy."
Rejoice with him, O heavens;
    bow down to him, all gods,
for he avenges the blood of his children
    and takes vengeance on his adversaries.
He repays those who hate him
    and cleanses his people's land.

As many have noted, the song's structure resembles the well-known ancient Near Eastern lawsuit, where a king or overlord accuses a vassal for breaking the treaty between them. The form involves, as McConville summarizes, "the call of witnesses, an accusation, an account of the overlord's benevolence, an affirmation that the covenant has been broken, and an announcement of punishment."[23] These features fit well with what we have in verses 2–25. What is so different here, however, is the final declaration of undeserved mercy at the end of this song. God

23. McConville, *Deuteronomy*, 451.

will punish his people (his vassal), but also his people's persecutor; and then, he will atone for the sins of the land and people. Habakkuk prayed that God, in his anger, would remember mercy (Hab. 3:2; cf. Ps. 30:5). What that prophet prayed, Moses sings about. This is why McConville says, "The Song is a witness, first of all, to the deep and abiding love of Yahweh for his people,"[24] and why Daniel Block labels this section "The Gospel."[25] Amid the horrors of judgment, hope shines forth![26]

The language used here is that of vengeance and vindication. Yes, God will judge all the people (those who call themselves "his people")[27] who scorn his salvation.[28] In fact, he will use the Canaanites as his "sword" (v. 41). But in due time that same sword will be turned around, piercing those who persecute. "Calamity" (v. 35) will come upon the Canaanites. God will recompense and then restore. "For the LORD will vindicate his people and have compassion on his servants" (v. 36).

Now, this mercy won't happen by some magical wave of the Mercy Wand—"I'm God and I say you're forgiven." No, the Lord will provide a cleansing or covering or atonement, as taught in the final verse (v. 43). As this song began with Moses calling the heavens to witness, so it ends by calling all creation to worship:

24. Ibid., 461.

25. Block, *Deuteronomy*, 1,125.

26. Earl S. Kalland notes that this song serves "both as a warning against disobedience and as a basis for hope when 'their strength is gone' (v. 36)." "Deuteronomy," in *Expositor's Bible Commentary*, ed. Frank E. Gaebelein, vol. 3 (Grand Rapids: Zondervan, 1992), 199.

27. Remember, as Paul taught in Romans 9–11, all Israel is not Israel. There is a remnant saved by grace through faith.

28. Matthew Henry describes verses 36–43 in this way: "A promise of the destruction of their enemies and oppressors at last, and the glorious deliverance of a remnant of Israel." *Matthew Henry's Commentary on the Whole Bible* (McLean, VA: MacDonald Publishing, 1985), 1:861.

Rejoice with him, O heavens;
  bow down to him, all gods,
for he avenges the blood of his children
  and takes vengeance on his adversaries.
He repays those who hate him
  and cleanses his people's land.

The heavens are called to rejoice over God's perfect, pure, and patient justice, but also over his great merciful cleansing.

The word translated "cleanses" here (*kipper* in Hebrew, as in Yom Kippur, the Day of Atonement; see Lev. 23:27) is most often translated "make atonement."[29] And this is why many translations render this last clause in verse 43, "He [God] will atone for his land and his people."[30] That's what's being said here. The picture is of God "clearing away and covering over the guilt" of his land and of his people.[31]

So the warning at the conclusion of this song, "Be careful to do all the words of this law," is set upon the foundation of God's act of salvation in the same way that the words of the Great Commission come at the end of Christ's saving event. After his life, passion, death, and resurrection, Jesus instructs his disciples to teach those who have been baptized "to observe all that I have commanded you" (Matt. 28:20). Atonement for sin is the motive—in Deuteronomy or Matthew or anywhere else in the Bible—to love and obey the one true God. Law doesn't bring about love, but love brings about a desire to keep the law, to obey God's word, to hold to his commands, which brings blessing and life.

The new covenant, which we are now under, is "new" and "better" than the old covenant. With Jesus as our perfect high

29. Exodus 30:10 is a good example: "Aaron shall *make atonement.* . . . With the blood of the sin offering of atonement he shall *make atonement.*"
30. This includes Block. See *Deuteronomy*, 1:126.
31. Thompson, *Deuteronomy*, 303–4.

priest, temple, and sacrifice, all the rules and rituals laid out in chapters 12–26 of Deuteronomy, for example, are indeed "obsolete" (Heb. 8:13). Yet don't forget the beautiful promise of the new covenant. What's unique about it? It is "not like the covenant" God made with those he brought "out of the land of Egypt," in that his "laws" are no longer written on stone tablets, but now are written upon "minds" and "hearts" (Heb. 8:8–10). The *Shema* is not on our foreheads, but in our heads. The command to love our neighbor is not printed over our doorpost, but housed in our hearts!

So then, does this mean that Christians can spiritually coast—put the internal law on cruise control, sit back, and let it drive us through the pearly gates? God forbid! There is a call that goes forth. This is how Revelation 14:12 puts it: "Here is a call for the endurance of the saints, those who keep the commandments of God and their faith in Jesus." The call is to faith and obedience, or what Paul terms at the beginning and end of Romans, "the obedience of faith" (1:5; 16:26).

## Warning Signs

Now, if God's Word tells us that we are to stay on the strait and narrow path, we would expect to find signs that point us in the direction we should go, and we would also expect to find warnings marking where we should not go. I don't know if you've come across these signs on your journey, but you should have, for they are everywhere in God's Word, especially in the New Testament: hold to the confession (Heb. 4:14), be doers of the word (James 1:22), be diligent to make your calling and election sure (2 Peter 1:10), work out your salvation with fear and trembling (Phil. 2:12). If we don't see and heed these, well then . . . watch out!

The book of Hebrews is filled with such warnings. It not only shows the superiority of the Son over Moses (which is interesting), but also contains a number of references to Deuteronomy 31–33 (of even more interest to our study!).[32] This shouldn't surprise us, since both Moses and the author of Hebrews are warning their generations about "the danger of apostasy."[33] Hebrews 1:6, for example, is a quotation from Deuteronomy 32:43 LXX, and Hebrews 10:30 a quotation from Deuteronomy 32:35–36.

Now it's the Hebrews 10 text which especially interests me, because it is so applicable to us. Hebrews 10:12–31 shows how the old and new come together as a kind of gentle wind, pushing us forward, or a soft rain, the analogy Moses uses, giving sustenance for growth. Starting in verse 12 (with my succinct commentary), we read:

> But when Christ had offered for all time a single sacrifice for sins, he sat down at the right hand of God, waiting from that time until his enemies should be made a footstool for his feet [that's atonement, full and perfect atonement; and that's what is being talked about in the highly visual details in Deut. 32:34–43]. For by a single offering he has perfected for all time those who are being sanctified. And the Holy Spirit also bears witness to us; for after saying [in Jer. 31:33], "This is the covenant that I will make with them

32. See R. Gheorghita, *The Role of the Septuagint in Hebrews. An Investigation of Its Influence with Special Consideration to the Use of Hab 2:3–4 in Hebrews 10:37–38*, WUNT 160 (Tübingen: Mohr Siebeck, 2003), 95. Referenced in Gert J. Steyn, "Deuteronomy in Hebrews," in *Deuteronomy in the New Testament*, ed. Menken and Moyise, 154. There Steyn notes, "It can be assumed that the Canticum Mosis was a familiar song among the Jews. Its presence amongst the Odes in Codex A of the LXX (at the end of the corpus of the Psalms) also points in this direction."

33. Steyn, "Deuteronomy in Hebrews," 157.

after those days, declares the Lord: I will put my laws on their hearts, and write them on their minds," then he adds [in Jer. 31:34], "I will remember their sins and their lawless deeds no more." [We are to remember God, but we can be thankful that he forgets our sins if we trust in Christ.] Where there is forgiveness of these, there is no longer any offering for sin. Therefore, brothers [here's our application!], since we have confidence to enter the holy places by the blood of Jesus, by the new and living way that he opened for us through the curtain, that is, through his flesh, and since we have a great priest over the house of God, let us draw near with a true heart in *full assurance of faith*, with our hearts sprinkled clean from an evil conscience and our bodies washed with pure water. [We have full assurance, along with full perseverance.] Let us hold fast the confession of our hope without wavering, for he who promised is faithful. And let us consider how to stir up one another to love and good works, not neglecting to meet together, as is the habit of some, but encouraging one another, and all the more as you see the Day drawing near. For if we go on sinning deliberately after receiving the knowledge of the truth ["deliberateness and continuance" is the key here—not that "the effect of Christ's sacrifice runs out," but rather that the persistent sinner runs away[34]], there no longer remains a sacrifice for sins, but a fearful expectation of judgment, and a fury of fire that will consume the adversaries. Anyone who has set aside the law of Moses dies without mercy on the evidence of two or three witnesses. How much worse punishment, do you think, will be deserved by the one who has spurned the Son of God, and has profaned the blood of the covenant by which he was sanctified, and has outraged the Spirit of grace? For we know him who said [in Deut. 32:35–36], "Vengeance is mine; I will repay." And again,

34. Hughes, *Hebrews*, 2:40.

"The Lord will judge his people." It is a fearful thing to fall into the hands of the living God.

How do Christians apply the Song of Moses most directly? Hebrews 10:12–31 tells us how. Do you hear the words of warning here? In verses 29–31, disobedience to the law of Moses is contrasted with spurning Jesus, profaning the blood of the new covenant, and outraging the Holy Spirit.[35] And notice who might fall into the hands of the living God, which is a fearful thing (v. 31): God's "people" might (v. 30), those who profess faith in Christ, who have been baptized (v. 22), who make it a habit to gather for worship (v. 25). And this is why the author of Hebrews warns us! Be careful. Don't play with this consuming fire. God's holiness is dangerous.

Be careful. But also be courageous: hold fast to the confession, stir one another up to love and good works, gather for worship, and stop sinning deliberately (vv. 23–26). You might say he says, "Be careful to do all the words of the law"—God's law, written by grace through faith upon our hearts.

## A Sign for All Times

When my wife and I lived in Hyde Park, near the University of Chicago, there was a chemistry professor who was part of our church. In his house he posted a strange sign above the inside doorway. In dark brown, bold, capital letters, it read, "REPENT." The sign blended nicely into the colors of the room, but its message was so abnormal in a domestic setting that it caused many a soul to pause and think. I suppose that message had the same effect

35. See Steyn, "Deuteronomy in Hebrews," 159.

on those who first heard it from the mouth of our Lord Jesus: "Repent, for the kingdom of God is at hand" (Mark 1:15). Those were the opening words of his ministry—words of warning.

Now, do you know what his last words were? We know the last words of Moses from this song and the blessing that follows in Deuteronomy 32–33, but what were the last words of Jesus? "Well," you say, "do you mean on the cross—where he said, 'Father, forgive them' and 'It is finished' and 'Into your hands I commend my spirit'? Or do you mean after the resurrection and before the ascension, where he spoke of the coming Spirit and the gospel witness going forth unto the ends of the earth (cf. Luke 24:46–49 and Acts 1:7–8)?" No, I mean the last words we find in the last book of the Bible, in Revelation 22, where Jesus says, "I am the root and the descendant of David, the bright morning star" (v. 16), and also, "Behold, I am coming quickly, and My reward is with Me, to render to every man according to what he has done" (v. 12, NASB). These "last words" of our Lord summarize, if you will, what's first in his heart. Like the Song of Yahweh, they warn us to be careful not to forget, and they warn us to be careful to obey—to live out the Word of God.

Then sang Deborah and Barak the son of Abinoam on that day:

² "That the leaders took the lead in Israel,
   that the people offered themselves willingly,
   bless the Lord!
³ Hear, O kings; give ear, O princes;
   to the Lord I will sing;
   I will make melody to the Lord, the God of Israel.
⁴ Lord, when you went out from Seir,
   when you marched from the region of Edom,
the earth trembled
   and the heavens dropped,
   yes, the clouds dropped water.
⁵ The mountains quaked before the Lord,
   even Sinai before the Lord, the God of Israel.
. . . . . . . . . . . . . . . . . . . . . . . . . . . . . . . . . . .

³¹ So may all your enemies perish, O Lord!
   But your friends be like the sun as he rises in his might."

And the land had rest for forty years. (Judg. 5:1–5, 31)

# 3

# The Song of Deborah:
# A Punctured Temple,
# a Pouring Out of Joy

⟨𝕄⟩

IN THE ART INSTITUTE of Chicago there hangs prominently Georges-Pierre Seurat's masterpiece, *A Sunday Afternoon
on the Island of La Grande Jatte*. In this work and others like it,
Seurat rejected the traditional method of oil painting (painting
broad brushstrokes of mixed color) and developed pointillism,
whereby he painstakingly applied tiny points of pure color upon
his canvas. The genius of this technique is this: when we view these
tiny juxtaposed dots of multicolored paint, our eyes automatically
blend the colors to form a picture. And so we see over here a boat
on the lake, and over there a child playing on the shore.

In this chapter, we set before our eyes the Song of Deborah,
and we find that it too is comprised of many little details—tiny
dots of color, if you will. If we look very closely, we see over
here Deborah the prophetess, who speaks the word of God, and

over there Barak, the military man of faith, and there behind them the armies of Israel—those who fought, and those who cowered—and all around them we see a storm and a slaughter, an assassination and a celebration. That's what we see up close. If we step back, however, an interesting thing happens—all these tiny points of color blend to form one dominant picture. It is a portrait of the Lord, a portrait of God triumphant!

## God Triumphs

Unlike military odes of the ancient Near East that celebrate with great exaggeration "superhuman achievements,"[1] the Song of Deborah, like Moses' two songs before it, exalts Yahweh as the primary hero.[2] We see this everywhere in this song, perhaps most notably in verses 2–4, which I think are a perfect snapshot of the whole:

> That the leaders took the lead in Israel,
>> that the people offered themselves willingly,
>> bless the Lord!
> Hear, O kings; give ear, O princes;
>> to the LORD I will sing;
>> I will make melody to the LORD, the God of Israel.
> LORD, when you went out from Seir,
>> when you marched from the region of Edom,
> the earth trembled
>> and the heavens dropped,
>> yes, the clouds dropped water.

1. Daniel I. Block, *Judges, Ruth*, NAC (Nashville: Broadman & Holman, 1999), 213.
2. Cf. Allan J. Hauser, "Two Songs of Victory: A Comparison of Exodus 15 and Judges 5," in *Directions in Biblical Hebrew Poetry*, ed. Elaine R. Follis (Sheffield: JSOT Press, 1987), 280.

In verse 2, Deborah acknowledges that Israel's leaders "took the lead" and also that her "people offered themselves willingly." Yet she acknowledges that God is ultimately to be praised for the victory—"Bless the LORD!" The real reason "the puny, ill-equipped Israelite force" defeated the large, well-equipped Canaanite army was that God called the whole of creation, if you will, to fulfill his will![3] Interestingly, as K. Lawson Younger Jr. observes, "not one single line of the poem shows the Israelites directly involved in the hard and dangerous work of warfare."[4] Even in verses 19–22, where we might expect something to be said of Israel's ten thousand gallant warriors, we find instead that, in Arthur Cundall's words, "the massed armies of the kings of the Canaanite city-states were met by the might of the forces of nature, *operating at the behest of Israel's God*."[5] God is "the One," as Younger puts it, "pulling the strings, raising generals, deploying armies . . . dictating strategy, and effecting the victory."[6] Thus, it is God, the one "who fights for you" (Josh. 23:10),[7] for whom Deborah reserves praise.

In verse 3, this theme of God-centered praise grows. Here, quite straightforwardly, Deborah calls upon all to offer worship as she does: "Hear, O kings; give ear, O princes; to the LORD I will sing; I will make melody to the LORD, the God of Israel." Then finally, in verse 4, we move from indirect to direct praise, as Deborah directly exalts and addresses God:

3. Arthur E. Cundall, *Judges: An Introduction and Commentary*, TOTC (Downers Grove, IL: InterVarsity, 1968), 95.

4. K. Lawson Younger Jr., *Judges and Ruth*, NIVAC (Grand Rapids: Zondervan, 2002), 153.

5. Cundall, *Judges*, 99 (emphasis added).

6. Younger, *Judges and Ruth*, 163.

7. As Cundall aptly states, "The difference made by a living faith in the living God is nothing less than sensational, and the words of Joshua, 'One man of you puts to flight a thousand, since it is the Lord your God who fights for you' (Josh. 23:10), were literally fulfilled on this occasion." *Judges*, 96.

"LORD, when you went out from Seir, when you marched from the region of Edom, the earth trembled and the heavens dropped, yes, the clouds dropped water." The God who descended onto Mount Sinai to reveal himself and his covenant with Israel (in the midst of a great storm, no less) is the same God who has again descended to deliver his people from those who oppose him and his will.[8] And the same God who is now flooding the Kishon River is the one who raised and lowered the waters of the Red Sea.[9]

## The Satellite View

As it is in verses 2–4, so it is throughout this song. The Lord is at the center, as is his victory. Let's turn our attention next to that victory. As the Canaanites, with their immense army, were poised for combat, suddenly a violent storm arose. This storm took them by surprise. (Ironically, they were Baal worshippers.)[10] Indeed, as these heavenly waters bombarded the earth, the Kishon River overflowed, sweeping them right into the army of Israel.

That's the ground footage. Here's the satellite view. It was the Lord who enlisted those very rain clouds in his army. And it was he, with the clouds and stars and the heavenly hosts, who

8. Ibid., 94; cf. C. F. Keil and F. Delitzsch, *Commentary on the Old Testament* (repr., Peabody, MA: Hendrickson, 2006), 2:224–25.
9. The flooding of the Kishon "echoes what happened to Pharaoh's armies" in the parting and falling of the Red Sea. Block, *Judges, Ruth*, 237.
10. Baal was the so-called god of storms and rain (see ibid., 223). Perhaps also, as Herbert Wolf notes, "the reference to the participation of the stars may be a slap at the astrological readings used by the Canaanites." "Judges," in *Expositor's Bible Commentary*, ed. Frank E. Gaebelein, vol. 3 (Grand Rapids: Zondervan, 1992), 414.

marched to war. It was the Lord, as Judges 4 (the narrative of this account) so clearly states, who routed (4:15) and subdued (4:23) the Canaanites and their king. It was the Lord who sat "enthroned over the flood" (Ps. 29:10; cf. 83:9).

You see, when you put all the little dots together, this is a portrait of God triumphant. The one, true, and living God is victorious in battle against his cosmic and his earthly enemies.

## God Triumphs in Righteousness

Now, such a portrait may be easy enough for us to recognize, but it may also be hard for us to appreciate. For some, this divine triumph leaves tension. Is this what God is really like?

Well, part of my task (like that of an art appreciation teacher) is to help you appreciate what is here, and so to see that what is seemingly grotesque is in fact sublimely beautiful. And the first point of clarification that will lead to appreciation is this: God triumphs in righteousness. Let me show you what I mean.

Most of us are familiar with the biblical concept of a holy war. Here in the Song of Deborah we have not only a holy war, but a *holy warrior*. In verses 10–11, all classes of Israelites, both the rich and the poor, as they are resting and refreshing themselves, are singing of God's victory. At the watering places, they are retelling the story of their salvation, what they call "the righteous triumphs of the LORD" (v. 11).

The Lord does not just triumph; he has righteous triumphs (cf. Pss. 129:4; 145:17). God is not some tyrant or some big bully who has without cause destroyed his enemies. Rather, God is strong, but sanctified; he is powerful, but pure; he is great, but good.[11]

---

11. With its fourfold repetition of God's goodness, Luiza Cruz's Spanish hymn, "Canta¡ Débora, Canta!" provides an apt summary.

Yes, most Christians will agree that God is good, that he is just in all he does. They will even concede that in this song and the battle it depicts, he is righteous. But I fear that too many believers believe this truth in their heads and not in their hearts. My aim here is to help you believe it in your heart.

## "It's Not Fair!"

My oldest daughter, when she was five, had a favorite phrase—"It's not fair." That was her response whenever a sibling got more of something than she did or got to do something that she couldn't. "It's not fair." That's what she said. And when I had neither the time nor the energy to give her a full explanation— you know, the imputation of Adam's sin and its effects upon the world—I would simply say, "Well, life isn't fair."

Life isn't fair—now that's not just the cry of a child, is it? No, we all cry out for justice! When we see and hear all that goes on around us, we want "a world put to rights," a world where the good guy always wins and the bad guy always loses.[12] Well, here in our text, the first fact I want you to see is that such justice prevails. The bad guys actually get what is coming to them.

The Bible makes clear that the Canaanites were an evil empire.[13] All the way back in chapter 15 of Genesis—before the

12. N. T. Wright, *Simply Christian: Why Christianity Makes Sense* (New York: HarperOne, 2006), 3.

13. "Do not say in your heart, after the LORD your God has thrust them out before you, 'It is because of my righteousness that the LORD has brought me in to possess this land,' whereas it is because of *the wickedness of these nations* that the LORD is driving them out before you. Not because of your righteousness or the uprightness of your heart are you going in to possess their land, but because of *the wickedness of these nations* the LORD your God is driving them out from before you, and that he may confirm the word that the LORD swore to your fathers, to Abraham, to Isaac, and to Jacob" (Deut. 9:4–5; cf. 18:9).

exodus, before Moses, and before Joshua—this evil is addressed. As God is making his covenant with Abraham, he speaks of the Amorites, which is just a code word for all the Canaanites. He says that the Egyptians will one day get it (as we saw in chapter 1 with the Song of Moses), and so will the Canaanites. But for now their iniquity "is not yet complete" (15:16). In other words, God is allowing evil to reach its boiling point. And by the time of Joshua and the judges, that point has been reached. So God, on the one hand, is ready to give the land to Israel, and on the other hand he is ready to judge the Canaanites—both in fulfillment of the patriarchal promises (cf. Deut. 9:3–6; Ps. 149:9).

Now, we can see these waters boiling over even in and around our text. In Judges 4:3 we read of Sisera, the commander of the Canaanite army, who "oppressed the people of Israel *cruelly* for twenty years." Then in the Song of Deborah we read of economic and spiritual oppression in verses 6–8, and of something even worse in verses 28–30. In the latter verses, we have further light shed on this heart of darkness. There we read of Sisera's mother—of her refined tastes, but unrefined conscience.

Sisera has been assassinated. But at home, unaware of this event, his mother waits. She is waiting for her mighty son to ride into town victoriously, as he has done so often before, with spoil—clothing as her plunder, people as his. As she lusts after "the richly embroidered dyed cloth" once worn by Israel's commanding officers,[14] her son, she suspects from previous experience, will lust after what's beneath the clothing of Israel's damsels—"a womb or two for every man," she says, speaking of the anticipated rape of the daughters of Israel.[15] It will all be part of their victory celebration.

14. Cundall, *Judges*, 101.
15. Wolf notes, "The word for 'girl' (*raham*, v. 30) normally means 'womb,' brusquely suggesting the lustful treatment each one could expect." *Judges*,

Now when older women talk this way about younger women, when "the ill-treatment which awaited the women-folk of a defeated army is passed over without any twinge of conscience or pity,"[16] we can safely say that the pot of evil has boiled over.

As much as we as a culture have become overly sympathetic to victim *and violator* alike, we still have not come so far as to lose our inward sense that such evils as these—cruel oppression, brutal rape, and senseless murder—should be dealt with. It is an interesting reality that the family of a murder victim always feels some sense of justice when the murderer is caught and punished. And we should have the same feeling when we read or sing this song. We ought to understand how the Israelites delighted in their deliverance from the Canaanites, which included delighting in the defeat and demise of evil (cf. Rev. 19:1–2).

Just as we found in Exodus 15, evil (the actual evil of the enemy) is one factor that helps us take God's *righteous* triumph to heart, to see this holy war and its holy warrior as actually holy—as good, pure, and righteous.

## Look in the Mirror

Another factor, beyond the evil of the enemy, is the evil in us, the evil that is in all of us. I think our biggest obstacle in seeing God as perfectly just (and thus able to mete out justice against those who oppose him) is our own failure to see ourselves as unjust.

---

416. Cundall calls the thought behind this word "contemptuous." *Judges*, 101. Younger gives a possible translation as "one or two broads/babes." *Judges and Ruth*, 156.

16. Cundall, *Judges*, 101.

Do you remember the time when the prophet Nathan confronted David after David's sins of adultery and murder—after he slept with Uriah's wife and then had that poor soldier sent to the front line to be killed in battle? Do you remember the story the prophet told (2 Sam. 12:1–7)? He said to the king (and I slightly paraphrase),

> There were two men in a certain city, the one rich and the other poor. The rich man had many flocks and herds, but the poor man had nothing but one little lamb, a lamb for which he saved up money and which he then bought. Now he raised this lamb, and it was like part of the family. It grew up with him and with his children. In fact, this lamb used to eat food from the poor man's hand and even drink from his cup. And at night it would lie in his arms. It was like a daughter to him. Now one day a traveler came to visit the rich man, and the rich man, concerned for his own wealth, was unwilling to take an animal from his own flock in order to prepare it as a meal for the guest. And so, do you know what he did instead? He took the poor man's lamb, and he killed it and he prepared it as a dinner for this visitor.

Now when David heard this report (he thought it was a report, not a tale), his anger, the Bible tells us, "was greatly kindled against the man, and he said to Nathan, 'As the LORD lives, the man who has done this deserves to die.'" Then Nathan, having made his point, said to David, "You are the man!"

We have a hard time worshipping God as a wrathful warrior who wars against the wicked because we have a hard time viewing ourselves as *the man*—the one who stands sinful before him, deserving to die. We have a hard time worshipping God as a righteous judge because we don't think we deserve his judgment.

We don't think we are as bad as the Bible says we are![17] You see, with so many trite evangelistic pleas given today—that Jesus will make you happy, that Jesus will heal your body, that Jesus will love you and be your best buddy, that Jesus will do and be this or that, all in the here and now (whatever the truth of some of it)—I fear we forget the central truth that Jesus saves us from the just judgment, from God's righteous wrath.

Have we forgotten that we, like Israel of old, were deserving of God's judgment, and that we, like them, were saved, not because we were more sanctified, but because God chose to have mercy, to rescue the unrighteous? Romans 5:6–10 makes this clear:

> For while we were still *weak*, at the right time Christ died for the *ungodly*. . . . God shows his love for us in that while we were still *sinners*, Christ died for us. Since, therefore, we have now been justified by his blood, much more shall we be saved by him *from the wrath of God*. For if while we were *enemies* we were reconciled to God by the death of his Son, much more, now that we are reconciled, shall we be saved by his life.

You can see how far removed we are from the mind of God that when we read the Song of Deborah or other texts like it, we immediately want to put God in the dock and say, "What's this all about? What's with all this warfare, this killing, this loss of life?" Or we ask, "Why are you so merciless?" Instead, we should ask him (who rightly sits behind the bench, and we in the dock), "Why are you so merciful?" He is merciful in judg-

17. Perhaps thinking of texts like John 2:24–25, C. S. Lewis remarks in *The Problem of Pain*: "Christ takes it for granted that men are bad." Quoted in Wayne Martindale and Jerry Root, eds., *The Quotable Lewis* (Carol Stream, IL: Tyndale, 1990), 157.

ing evil and evildoers, and merciful in not judging this evil and this evildoer.

Skeptics sometimes scoff, "If God is so good, why then doesn't he deal with all evil right now?" The apostle Peter, a one-time skeptic himself, has much to say to such scoffing. In that splendid second letter of his, he gives this reply: "The Lord is not slow to fulfill his promise as some count slowness [in other words, your timing is not his timing, his justice will let roll when it lets roll], but [here's why he's so slow, so to speak: because he] is patient toward you, not wishing that any should perish, but that all should reach repentance" (2 Peter 3:9). If God dealt with evil, each and every evil, he would also have to deal with you. And are you ready for him to deal with you?

> Mine eyes have seen the glory of the coming of the Lord;
> He is trampling out the vintage where the grapes of wrath
>     are stored;
> He hath loosed the fateful lightning of His terrible swift sword.[18]

Judgment is coming at God's perfect pace. But, oh how gracious God is, so patient, that he wants even you to reach something—and it's not your full potential. No, He wants you to "reach repentance."

As strange as this may sound, this *gory song of glory*—Deborah's song of the Canaanites getting theirs—is in fact a kind of gracious invitation, an invitation for the sinner to repent. No time for repentance is offered to the Canaanites. But such a time is now offered to you.

The Bible is full of pictures of judgment—whether it is Noah and the flood or the Tower of Babel or Sodom and Gomorrah or the plagues and the Passover or all those vivid images in

---

18. From Julia Ward Howe's hymn "The Battle Hymn of the Republic."

Revelation of the lake of fire and so on. And here in the Song of Deborah we have another picture of judgment for all who oppose God. All of these pictures are but gracious warnings. They are merciful invitations to come to Christ, the one mediator between holy God and sinful man (1 Tim. 2:5). God is slow to anger; he does not rush to wrath. He is slow to anger, but quick (ever so quick!) to forgive any and all who come to his Son in repentance and faith.

## God Triumphs through Weakness

So, *God triumphs in righteousness*—do you know that in your head? And do you know it also in your heart? The other theological truth of this text that we should know in both head and heart is that *God triumphs through weakness*.

In the Seurat painting, the one I mentioned earlier, there is much to see and contemplate. There's the island itself and the water that surrounds it. Then there are all the people—nearly fifty men, women, and children. The largest person in this painting is a well-dressed woman. She is likely the one whom you see first. And at her feet is a pet monkey. Yes, a pet monkey! This little monkey is on a leash, but poised to jump on a dog, who is unleashed, and who is running but inches away from it.

In the Song of Deborah, there is likewise much to see and contemplate. We could meditate upon the land and the water or upon all the persons involved, especially Deborah and Barak. I want us to focus, however, on a seemingly less significant character, one we find in verses 24–27. For here beneath the feet, if you will, of the foremost character (who is the Lord), we find one creature on the leash of God's providence, so to speak, a creature who is about to pounce upon a running dog. Her name is Jael.

Similar to the "unrestrained praise" Elizabeth gave to to Mary in Luke's gospel,[19] verse 24 begins, "Most blessed of women be Jael, the wife of Heber the Kenite, of tent-dwelling women most blessed." Now, why is she so blessed—this non-Israelite, this woman? Well, here's the story, told in chapter 4 and retold poetically here in verses 25, 26, and 27:

> He asked water and she gave him milk;
>   she brought him curds in a noble's bowl.
> She sent her hand to the tent peg
>   and her right hand to the workmen's mallet;
> she struck Sisera;
>   she crushed his head;
>   she shattered and pierced his temple.
> Between her feet
>   he sank, he fell, he lay still;
> between her feet
>   he sank, he fell;
>   where he sank, there he fell—dead.

Well, isn't that pleasant? Murder. What a lovely sin to sing about! It is one thing to explain God as a warrior, but how shall we explain this? How are we to get our heads, let alone our hearts, around this one—Israel's joy over Jael?

Here's how. I want you to think of the Canaanites as an ancient version of the Third Reich and of Sisera as a kind of Adolph Hitler, for he was that kind of powerful and diabolical political figure. Finally, think of Jael as a young Polish woman whose land has been taken after the German invasion. She is loyal to the Reich, as is her town, but only by default, as a matter of survival.

19. Younger, *Judges and Ruth*, 154.

Now, Hitler and his army have just suffered great loss. His army has been slaughtered. As he is fleeing on foot, he sees and enters her home, for him a place of safety (because her husband had made a peace treaty with him, see 4:11). And then, being so weary from battle and from flight, he asks for water (which, ironically, just destroyed his army!) and lies down to rest. But instead of bringing water, she brings milk, which mixed with his great exhaustion quickly sedates him. He falls into deep sleep.

The camera lens subtly sweeps across the room from him to her. He is fast asleep. She is wide awake. Her heart is pounding. What should she do? And what will she do? What would you do? This "Hitler" is so close at hand. Will she play it safe, like some of the tribes of Israel did, or will she stand idly by, as the inhabitants of Meroz did, and allow the fleeing enemy to escape (v. 23),[20] or will she risk everything?

The camera closes in on her. Her left hand reaches for an ordinary tent peg, her right hand for a hammer. She walks over to Sisera, softly, ever so "softly" (4:21). She moves the peg near his temple. And she pounds, one swift, deadly blow. And between her feet he sinks, he falls; he sinks, he falls; he sinks, he falls—dead.[21]

20. Younger notes, "Meroz did not aid Yahweh in the pursuit; but Jael, the wife of a Kenite did, and she is praised (lit. 'blessed') as fervently as Meroz is cursed. In a sense, Meroz represents those Israelites who have taken their stand on the side of the Canaanites; Jael (in the next stanza) represents those non-Israelites who have taken their stand on the side of Israel." Ibid., 154.

21. I concur with many commentators that the poetry here is "magnificent, featuring many examples of climactic (repetitive) parallelism (vv. 7, 19–20, 27) and onomatopoeia (v. 22)." Wolf, *Judges*, 408 and 413. See especially M. D. Coogan, "A Structural and Literary Analysis of the Song of Deborah," *CBQ* 40 (1978): 143–66. Block adds, "Verse 27 offers one of the most impressive examples of staircase parallelism in the Old Testament." *Judges, Ruth*, 241. And, Younger notes how, in the Hebrew, verse 27 "describes the action with a tantalizingly slow sequence of verbs that present his 'fall.'" *Judges and Ruth*, 155.

# Mighty Men

When I taught a class on medieval literature, one of the classics we read was *The Song of Roland*. This is an epic poem which embellishes a relatively minor military incident of the eighth century. In the poem, Roland is ambushed by the enemy and left for dead. But before he dies, he blows his horn heroically, and it sounds so loudly that it reaches the ears of Charlemagne many miles away. So Charlemagne, the Holy Roman Emperor, rides into town and quickly wipes out the enemy.

As much as *The Song of Roland* is embellished, it does give us a normal perspective on military victories and military heroes. Military heroes do have a certain power and prowess about them. They are like Charlemagne—mighty men! Well, here in the Song of Deborah, as the prophetess herself predicted—"the LORD will sell Sisera into the hand of a woman" (4:9; cf. 9:54)—the mightiest man has fallen into the hand of a woman. Sisera, who was supposed to bring home many women captive to prey upon, has himself been preyed upon by a woman. The destroyer is destroyed. The hunter is hunted. The killer is killed. The dog is dead.

Now, can you begin to see why I have labeled the second section of this chapter "God Triumphs through Weakness"? The instrument of his justice is not Barak, Israel's valiant warrior. It is no warrior at all, but a woman.[22] It is an ordinary housewife,

22. Recently I read Mary Gordon's biography, *Joan of Arc* (New York: Viking, 2000). Gordon begins by recounting her shock at witnessing two girls fighting in public. One girl, she recalls, threw the other to the ground, straddled her, and then hit her in the face (p. xvii). To Gordon, as it would be to most of us, the sight of girls or even women in hand-to-hand combat is shocking to our sensibilities. This is one reason why she emphatically states of Joan, "There is no one like her" (p. xix). A similar shock should hit us as we read, not only about Deborah's involvement in this battle, but also and especially about Jael. Jael's action, mainly because of her gender,

a very unlikely hero.[23] And in this way, with this story within this song (and with this most ironic twist in a series of ironic twists), Israel is praising and God is proving what he proves many times over: he uses the weaker things (or what the world considers the weaker things) to confound the wise and to conquer the mighty.[24]

God is triumphant. God is triumphant in righteousness. God is triumphant through weakness. As we step back from this text, that is the portrait we see painted here.

## Putting the Pieces Together

My middle daughter, when she was very young, loved putting puzzles together. She had and still has a real knack for it. When she was just three years old, it was fun for me (having put together fewer than ten puzzles in my entire life) to see her little mind and fingers hard at work, figuring out how each piece fitted into the next. It was also fun, as she advanced from twenty-five-piece puzzles up to seventy-five- and then one-hundred-piece puzzles, to see—by the way she laid everything out and started and finished the puzzle—how

should be just as shocking as two girls fighting in public or a medieval maiden wielding a sword and wearing heavy armor.

23. Younger says, "Finally, Jael emerges as the real heroine of the narrative. But this is ironic too. She is hardly an orthodox hero. Rather, she shares the unorthodox qualities of Ehud and Shamgar. Like Ehud, Jael is a lone assassin. . . . Moreover, like Shamgar, Jael is a non-Israelite. . . . Her action is morally ambiguous, but her courage and the sheer virtuosity of her performance are sufficient to silence criticism on that score (5:24). The crowning aspect of her unorthodoxy as a hero is her sex: Yahweh sells Sisera into the hand of a woman." *Judges and Ruth*, 146. Block also notes, "But individually the highest accolades go to two women, Deborah and Jael, whose courage and sagacity won the day for Israel. The feminine motif is obvious and intentional." *Judges, Ruth*, 217.

24. Younger, *Judges and Ruth*, 159.

she figured out some of the predictable patterns, how she grasped the way puzzles work.

There is also a way in which the Bible works. Sometimes the Bible gives us straightforward prophecies—this will be then, and then will be that. But at other times the Bible gives us patterns, patterns of the way in which God works, patterns that become all the more predictable, the more you read along.

One of the patterns that emerges is the pattern of God triumphing in righteousness and yet through weakness. So if you've been reading through your Bible and picking up on this pattern (solving, if you will, all these twenty-five-piece puzzles), then you see it here in the Song of Deborah, and there in the life of David, and so on. Well, when you come to the Gospels (let's call those the one-hundred-piece puzzles of the Bible) and you see the depiction of Jesus and watch him walk to the cross, and there give his life away, you should say to yourself, "Oh yes, I see! That makes perfect sense. It fits!" It fits the pattern. In the cross of Christ, God triumphs in righteousness; he triumphs through weakness.

You see, the Old Testament makes us wise unto salvation because it convicts us of our sin and also because it points us to a savior, a Savior who triumphs in righteousness through weakness, the one in whom we ought to place our faith.

My mouth derides my enemies,
  because I rejoice in your salvation.
² There is none holy like the Lᴏʀᴅ;
  there is none besides you;
  there is no rock like our God.
. . . . . . . . . . . . . . . . . . . . .

For this I will praise you, O Lᴏʀᴅ, among the nations,
  and sing praises to your name.
⁵¹ Great salvation he brings to his king,
  and shows steadfast love to his anointed,
  to David and his offspring forever.
      (1 Sam. 2:1b–2; 2 Sam. 22:50–51)

# 4

# The Songs in Samuel: The Barren Woman and the Fertile King

THE IRISH POET Seamus Heaney, in his brilliant and tragic poem "Mid-Term Break," writes of what is for many our greatest fear and for some their deepest sorrow—the death of a child:

> I sat all morning in the college sick bay
> Counting bells knelling classes to a close.
> At two o'clock our neighbors drove me home.
>
> In the porch I met my father crying—
> He had always taken funerals in his stride—
> And Big Jim Evans saying it was a hard blow.
>
> The baby cooed and laughed and rocked the pram
> When I came in, and I was embarrassed
> By old men standing up to shake my hand

And tell me they were "sorry for my trouble."
Whispers informed strangers I was the eldest,
Away at school, as my mother held my hand

In hers and coughed out angry tearless sighs.
At ten o'clock the ambulance arrived
With the corpse, stanched and bandaged by the nurses.

Next morning I went up into the room. Snowdrops
And candles soothed the bedside; I saw him
For the first time in six weeks. Paler now,

Wearing a poppy bruise on the left temple,
He lay in the four foot box as in a cot.
No gaudy scars, the bumper knocked him clear.

A four foot box, a foot for every year.[1]

In the ancient world, and especially for a woman in ancient
Israel, the closest emotional equivalent to having to bury a son
was never to have one. Hannah hadn't had one. And so it is with
her barrenness, and the emotional intensity that accompanies it,
that the book of 1 Samuel begins. We learn of childless Hannah,
who coughs out, not "angry tearless sighs," but faithful tearful
cries. "Hannah, why do you weep? And why do you not eat?
And why is your heart sad?" her husband asks (1:8). She cries
because the Lord has "closed her womb" (1:5–6).

The first chapter of 1 Samuel begins with the plight, promise,
and praise of Hannah. Her *plight* is her barrenness. Her *promise*
is that if God will give her a son, she will "give him to the LORD
all the days of his life" (v. 11). Finally, we have her *praise*. When

---

1. Seamus Heaney, *Opened Ground: Select Poems 1966–1996* (New York: Farrar, Strauss and Giroux, 1998), 11.

Samuel is born, she acknowledges and worships the Lord for remembering her (vv. 19– 20; cf. Ps. 113:9).

So, her plight, promise, and praise—that's chapter 1. Her *prayer*—that's chapter 2, the first ten verses. Here, as she sings in celebration of the Lord, we have what is often regarded as Hannah's hymn,[2] a song which sings of the way God worked in the past (vv. 1–2), works in the present (vv. 3–8), and will work in the future (vv. 9–10).

## The Way the Lord Worked

Starting with verses 1–2, we hear of the way the Lord worked. Hannah sings,

My heart exults in the LORD;
    my strength is exalted in the LORD.
My mouth derides my enemies,
    because I rejoice in your salvation.
There is none holy like the LORD;
    there is none besides you;
    there is no rock like our God.

Here there are three words I want us to focus on because they summarize the themes of this song. First we have the word

2. Ronald F. Youngblood notes, "Although 1 Samuel 2:1–10 is a prayer . . . it is commonly referred to as the 'Song of Hannah' because of its lyrical qualities and similarities to other ancient OT hymns (e.g., the Song of Moses and Miriam, Exod 15:1–18, 21; the Song of Moses, Deut 32:1–43; the Song of Deborah, Judg 5; and esp. the Song of David, 2 Sam 22)." "1 & 2 Samuel," in *Expositor's Bible Commentary*, ed. Frank E. Gaebelein, vol. 3 (Grand Rapids: Zondervan, 1992), 578. Cf. P. Kyle McCarter Jr., *1 Samuel*, AB (New York: Doubleday, 1979), 75. I would also add the similarities with Habakkuk's "prayer" (Hab. 3:1) which was made into a song (see 3:19). Perhaps this explains why Mary knew the Song of Hannah and used it as the model of her prayer/song (Luke 1:46–55).

"LORD" (Yahweh). Forty-six times in the first two chapters of 1 Samuel, we find God's covenantal name. In our text, the name appears three times. This song is sung to the Lord and about the Lord. Here Hannah exalts Yahweh for his salvation, holiness, uniqueness, and strength. Later she will add his knowledge, justice, and sovereignty. Thus, once again, similar to the songs of Moses and Deborah, we have a God-centered song.

The second word we should notice is the first person pronoun "my" (and with that, "I"). Interestingly, this song is God-centered, but it is also self-centered. Well, not self-centered in a bad sense, but self-expressive or *personal*. Hannah says, "My heart . . . my strength . . . my mouth . . . my enemies . . . I rejoice" (v. 1).

I have read the lyrics of thousands of contemporary praise choruses, and I have observed, as have many others, a certain self-centeredness in them. In fact, my study of the top songs sung in American churches between February 2000 and August 2008 (see the appendix) revealed that the words *I, me,* and *my* dominate the titles and lyrics of these songs. Sadly, even in good lyrics like "Jesus died for me," the focus falls not on Jesus or his death, but rather on "me." Yet, however these contemporary songs may be critiqued,[3] it does not diminish the abundance and thus the significance of the first person pronoun in this song or in the scriptural songs in general. So, while today's church may sing, "Jesus loves me," stressing the words in reverse order, the clear witness and proper focus of the scriptural songs remains.

Do you remember how the songs of Moses began? "*I* will sing to the LORD" (Ex. 15:1). "The LORD is *my* strength and *my* song, and he has become *my* salvation" (v. 2). "Give ear, O heavens, and *I* will speak, and let the earth hear the words of *my*

3. For a fuller critique, see chapter 7.

mouth. May *my* teaching drop as the rain. . . . For *I* will proclaim the name of the Lord; ascribe greatness to our God!" (Deut. 32:1–3). The Song of Deborah is nearly identical. Deborah waits for the second line of her song to say, "To the Lord *I* will sing; *I* will make melody to the Lord" (Judg. 5:3). The Psalms are little different. In Israel's inspired songbook, from which Paul twice exhorts Christians to sing (Eph. 5:19; Col. 3:16), we again find all those "me's" and "my's" and "I's." Think of the beginning of Psalm 23, "The Lord is *my* shepherd; *I* shall not want," or the beginning of Psalm 18:

> *I* love you, O Lord, *my* strength.
> The Lord is *my* rock and *my* fortress and *my* deliverer,
>  *my* God, *my* rock, in whom *I* take refuge,
> *my* shield, and the horn of *my* salvation, *my* stronghold.
> *I* call upon the Lord, who is worthy to be praised,
>  and *I* am saved from *my* enemies.[4]

So, the problem is not the use of the first person pronoun, as many music critics claim. Rather, it is self-love lyrics! There is a subtle but significant difference between "the Lord exults in my heart" and "My heart exults in the Lord." The latter perfectly balances personal references with praise for God.

## The Lord Is My Salvation

"Lord" is the first key word in the Song of Hannah, and "my" is the second. The third word is "salvation." We find this important word in 1 Samuel 2:1, where Hannah sings, "I rejoice in your salvation." Dale Ralph Davis, in his fine commentary,

---

4. For a plethora of person pronouns, see Psalm 25:16–21.

SERMONS ON THE SONGS

labels the salvation of which she sings here a "micro-salvation," as opposed to the "macro-salvation" in verses 9–10.[5] What he means is that in verses 1–2 Hannah is expressing her elation over a particular deliverance—in this case, from her barrenness. This sense of salvation is best supported by the immediate context. In verse 1, Hannah speaks of her "enemies," who were those who ridiculed her for her barrenness. So here Hannah sings of her salvation, one might say (to borrow Pauline terminology), "through childbearing" (1 Tim. 2:15). It is this micro or smaller salvation which first occupies her mind.

A few months before I was saved, I was saved. That is, before God graciously spared my soul, he spared my life. A friend and I loaded and hitched a trailer very improperly. We loaded a bunch of extremely heavy folding tables all on one side. This created, as we soon discovered, a potentially deadly imbalance. On the backstreets, we noticed nothing. The van moved slowly and safely straight ahead, the trailer dutifully following behind. But when we entered the Eisenhower Expressway and increased our speed, the trailer started to sway back and forth. Finally, it lifted up the front of the van, causing me to lose control of the wheel. In the middle of heavy traffic, the van did a 180, as we whipped around from the outside lane all the way to the inside shoulder, spinning and skidding rapidly across three lanes. I knew we would get hit. I braced myself, as I pumped the brakes. We stopped three inches before the concrete divider—untouched.

Now, I clearly remember the song that was blaring on the radio during all this swaying, spinning, and stopping. It was the

5. Dale Ralph Davis, *1 Samuel: Looking on the Heart*, FOB (Fearn, Ross-shire, UK: Christian Focus, 2000), 18–19. For other examples of songs based on "small salvations," see Numbers 21:17–18 (praising God for his provision of water in the desert) and Isaiah 38:9ff., notably verse 20 (Hezekiah's prayer about his recovery of health), and possibly Jonah 2:7, 10 (if it was composed after the Lord spared Jonah's life).

once popular rock ballad "Don't Stop Believing." Well, the fact was I hadn't yet started believing. I hadn't yet started believing in Jesus as my Lord and Savior. I was spiritually dead, and if I had died that day, I would have died in my sins. But no! God saved me. Yes, it was just a small salvation compared to the one that would come a few months later, but it was a very real salvation nevertheless.

Do you have such stories in your life? And do you thank God for your small salvations, all those times he has saved you in one way or another—from a sin, from a wrong relationship, from a bad job, from scorn, from death? Hannah did. She praised God for the way he worked, the specific way he worked in her life.

## The Way the Lord Works

Hannah starts with herself and her personal salvation in this song, but she does not dwell on it. Her view quickly expands to see not only the way God has worked in her life, but the way he works *generally* to provide justice in this world. This she describes in verses 3–8.

Now here, instead of looking for a few key words as we just did, I want us to walk backward through these six verses. This is not because I have found some hidden meaning, as many have done by playing Beatles' records in reverse. Rather, it is because I have found this to be the logical and theological flow. I think you'll see what I'm getting at as you walk with me.

So, come with me to the last sentence of verse 8. There we read, "For the pillars of the earth are the LORD's, and on them he has set the world." Here's the theological foundation of all that comes before it. Here we are told that God has sovereignly "set the world," and that all its "pillars" are under the power of his providence.

Moving backward, we come to verses 6–8a. Here the important detail to note is that God is the subject (the one acting):

> The LORD kills and brings to life;
>     he brings down to Sheol and raises up.
> The LORD makes poor and makes rich;
>     he brings low and he exalts.
> He raises up the poor from the dust;
>     he lifts the needy from the ash heap
> to make them sit with princes
>     and inherit a seat of honor.

So that's the way the Lord works in the world. Next, take another step back, back to verses 4–5, and notice how God's working in the world works out in people's lives. Notice also how the subject has changed from God to people (although God is still assumed to be the primary cause):

> The bows of the mighty are broken,
>     but the feeble bind on strength.
> Those who were full have hired themselves out for bread,
>     but those who were hungry have ceased to hunger.
> The barren has borne seven,
>     but she who has many children is forlorn.

It is easy enough to see that these verses (vv. 4–8) speak of divine reversals of fortune. But it is perhaps not all that easy to understand what the point of all this is. Well, we are getting there. With two more small steps backward, we'll find our answer. Look at the second half of verse 3: "The LORD is a God of knowledge, and by him actions are weighed." Ah, God sees all and judges all. Now we take our last step, reaching the first half of verse 3: "Talk no more so very proudly, let not arrogance come from your mouth."

So think of it this way. Our application of verses 1–2 should be: Open our mouths! Like Hannah, let us open our mouths in praise to God for salvation. Yet our application of verses 3–8 should be the opposite: Close our mouths. That is, do not be proud and do not boast. Why? The reason is simple. The famous proverb puts it perfectly: "Pride goes before a fall" (cf. Prov. 16:18)—or, conversely, humility comes before exaltation. That's what's being talked about here.

Have you ever been around an extremely arrogant person? I remember when I was working on a sermon in a coffeehouse, and at the table next to me was a man in whom pride poured out of his pores, or at least flowed from his mouth. He was a young man (perhaps twenty-one), and he was sitting with a slightly younger woman (perhaps the problem). He would boastfully name various professors with whom he was acquainted and make some statement about them to her. But when she would say something positive about these cerebral celebrities or what they had written, he would reply with something negative about them, such as, "Well, yes, but did you know . . ." or "Just the other day I was talking to him, and he told me . . ." Do you see what he was doing? He was using these people to lift himself up. But then, when this woman said something that made them higher up than he, he felt it necessary to knock them down a bit. So, either way, he would rise to the top.

This man was probably oblivious to what he was doing. I'm sure he was blind to his boasting and his pride. But you know what? So are a lot of us. Sometimes we are oblivious to what we are really saying. In some ways, this man repulsed me; in other ways, he reminded me of myself. It was as if he had mirrors on his clothing and on his face and his tongue, for in him, to some extent, was my reflection—and, I can safely say, yours as well. Pride is the mother of all sins, and there is a bit of her DNA in all of us. And so Hannah's exhortation is our application: We must always be on guard with what we say and how we say it, for the proud fall and the humble rise.

## The Way the Lord *Will* Work

Having looked at the way the Lord worked (vv. 1–2) and also at the way the Lord works (vv. 3–8), we arrive at the way the Lord will work in verses 9–10. Notice the future tense:

> He will guard the feet of his faithful ones,
>> but the wicked shall be cut off in darkness,
>> for not by might shall a man prevail.
> The adversaries of the LORD shall be broken to pieces;
>> against them he will thunder in heaven.
> The LORD will judge the ends of the earth;
>> he will give strength to his king
>> and exalt the power of his anointed.

This whole hymn resembles a handheld telescope, with verses 1–2 as the eyepiece, verses 3–8 the tube, and verses 9–10 the objective lens (the part that magnifies the image). As Hannah looks through the eyepiece of her smaller salvation, and through the tube of God's general justice, she sees now, out the end of this telescope, in the distant future, a full and final salvation. And do you see what she sees? There are three images. First, she sees God's protection of the righteous: "He will guard the feet of his faithful ones." Second, she sees God's punishment of the wicked: "But the wicked shall be cut off in darkness." Third, she sees God's empowerment of his Christ: "He will give strength to his king and exalt the power of his anointed."[6]

One of the questions I've been asking myself as I study these Songs of Scripture is this: how is this song *similar* to and how is it *different* from the songs which precede it? The Song of Hannah is similar to the songs of Moses and the Song of Deborah in five ways. First, it is God-centered. Second, it sings of salvation. Third, it mentions enemies and the justice coming to them. Fourth, it is personal. Fifth, it connects God's work with nature or creation—for example, "God will thunder in heaven."[7]

There are two major differences. First, we have in the Song of Hannah an emphasis on the reversal of fortunes. The Song of Deborah hints at this, but the Song of Hannah stresses it! Second, and most importantly, the Song of Hannah speaks of the Anointed One, of the coming of Christ.

So as Hannah is looking through her telescope, through the eyepiece and the tube, she sees up close the figure of a man. She sees a king. Now as she adjusts the eyepiece (I'm told it's called a focuser), the first figure she focuses on is Saul. Saul is the people's choice for king. He is the king after Israel's heart (1 Sam. 8:4–6, 19–20; 9:1ff.). Well, Saul doesn't fare so well, does he? So he soon falls out of focus. But then, with a slight adjustment, she sees David. Yes, David, the king after God's own heart (1 Sam. 13:14)!

6. C. F. Keil notes: "Acquainted as she was with the destination of Israel to be a *kingdom*, from the promises which God had given to the patriarchs, and filled as she was with the longing that had been awakened in the nation for the realization of these promises, she could see in spirit, and through the inspiration of God, the *king* whom the Lord was about to give to His people, and through whom He would raise it up to might and dominion." C. F. Keil and F. Delitzsch, *Commentary on the Old Testament* (repr., Peabody, MA: Hendrickson, 2006), 2:381; cf. p. 384 and the comment about Hannah's "prophetic glance."

7. If not for Deuteronomy 32, we could add a sixth similarity: all of these songs were sung by women—Miriam, Deborah, and Hannah.

Let's keep our sights on David for just a moment. David is important! His importance is stressed in the Bible a number of ways, perhaps most notably by the fact that his name is referenced over 1,000 times, which is the most of any human being.

The book of Judges whets our appetite for David. Its refrain and final verdict is: "In those days there was no king in Israel. Everyone did what was right in his own eyes" (Judg. 21:25). Then, the book of Ruth plants the seed of David. The very last verse in Ruth is the most important: "Obed fathered Jesse, and Jesse fathered David." In Hebrew, as in English, "David" is the last word. Finally, 1 and 2 Samuel tell us the story of the rise of this king and his kingdom. I think of these three books in this way:

Judges: There is no king.
Ruth: Here comes the king.
1 and 2 Samuel: Here is the king!

Now, if we unroll the scroll of 1 and 2 Samuel—which was originally one book, not two—we discover something quite interesting. We find not only what scholars call an *inclusio*, but also an important thematic development. At the beginning of the scroll, we have the Song of Hannah (1 Sam. 2), and at the end the Song of David (2 Sam. 22). These are both praise songs (or even "love" songs; cf. Ps. 18),[8] and they begin

8. Psalm 18, which is nearly identical with 2 Samuel 22, adds the words "I love you, O LORD, my strength" at the beginning (v. 1). It also concludes with a note on God's covenant love to David (v. 50). In other words, it shows why David loves God and why God loves David, his anointed. While the command to "love the LORD" is used as a summary of Israel's covenantal commitment (see Deut. 6:5; 11:1, 13; 13:3; Josh. 22:5; cf. Matt. 22:37), it is a rare expression for devotional poetry (possible exceptions might be Pss. 31:23; 97:10; 116:1; cf. Eph. 6:24).

with similar language—speaking of God's strength with the metaphor of a "horn"—and end with the theme of salvation through the king or anointed one (cf. 1 Sam. 2:1 and 2 Sam. 22:3), but the latter song functions as a partial fulfillment of the former one.

I say "partial" because the rise of David to power is incomplete. Hannah prays for a divinely empowered king who will establish a final justice, one which extends unto the ends of the earth. David is not that king. While the end of his song celebrates the fact that God has given him "vengeance and brought down peoples under [him]" (v. 49), the focus falls more on God's rescue and protection of David for the sake of his offspring, as the last verse testifies—"Great salvation he brings to his king, and shows steadfast love to his anointed, to David and his offspring forever."

In 2 Samuel 22:5–20, David simply elaborates on the theme of deliverance from the hands of his enemies (see vv. 2–4). Here he reflects upon a lifetime of such divine interventions.[9] He relives his many God-given escapes and victories.[10] He relives the dramatic getaways and deliverances from the clutches of crazed King Saul. He relives the numerous military victories God allotted him against Israel's enemies. He even relives the bittersweet salvation he obtained from the hand of his rebellious son, Absalom. He relives how the God who saved a small shepherd boy from the mighty arm of Goliath is the same God who has brought to him his kingly reign and the promise of an eternal kingdom through his offspring.[11] But he does not relive

9. See James Montgomery Boice, *Psalms* (Grand Rapids: Baker, 1994–98), 1:46.

10. Derek Kidner, *Psalms 1–72*, TOTC (Downers Grove, IL: InterVarsity, 1973), 91.

11. "When your days are fulfilled and you lie down with your fathers, I will raise up your offspring after you, who shall come from your body, and I will establish his

how he subdued all his enemies under his foot or how the whole world is under his dominion. The king who will do that, he knows, is yet to come.

After David comes Solomon, his son. Solomon amasses much wisdom, wealth, and power. Yet Solomon, as we know, is not the one. He rises and falls, as do all the rest of the kings in Israel and in Judah.

But the exilic prophets come along and renew the hope of this promise. Jeremiah, for example, says, "Behold, the days are coming, declares the LORD, when I will raise up for David a righteous Branch, and he shall reign as king and deal wisely, and shall execute justice and righteousness in the land" (Jer. 23:5). (Sounds like Hannah, doesn't he?) And Isaiah writes, "Of the increase of his government and of peace there will be no end, on the throne of David and over his kingdom, to establish it and to uphold it with justice and with righteousness from this time forth and forevermore" (Isa. 9:7).

## The Son of David

So, picture Hannah again, looking through her telescope. She sees David. She sees Solomon. She sees a good king here and a bad king there. Then her vision is blurred. She can't make out anything or anyone. But then she refocuses the focuser a touch, and then a touch more. And now she sees an angel coming into focus (very distant from her). Why, it's the angel Gabriel! He is announcing something of great importance to a young virgin betrothed to a man named Joseph, a man from the house or lineage of David (Luke 1:26). The angel says to her:

---

kingdom. He shall build a house for my name, and I will establish the throne of his kingdom forever" (2 Sam. 7:12–13).

Do not be afraid, Mary, for you have found favor with God. And behold, you will conceive in your womb and bear a son, and you shall call his name Jesus. He will be great and will be called the Son of the Most High. And the Lord God will give to him the throne of his father David, and he will reign over the house of Jacob forever, and of his kingdom there will be no end. (Luke 1:30–33)

Then Mary sings, in her Magnificat (which is an embellishment of Hannah's song),[12] "My soul magnifies the Lord . . . for he has looked on the humble estate of his servant" (Luke 1:46–48). Then Zechariah, the father of John the Baptist, joins in her chorus of praise, singing, "Blessed be the Lord God of Israel, for he has visited and redeemed his people and has raised up a horn of salvation for us in the house of his servant David" (1:68–69).

How does the New Testament open? It opens with these words: "The book of the genealogy of Jesus Christ, the son of David" (Matt. 1:1). That's right. David! And how then does it close? As we saw in chapter 2, it very nearly closes with these words: "I, Jesus . . . am the root and the descendant of David" (Rev. 22:16). And what do we find in between those first and last words? Why we find, in Jesus' own words, "something greater

---

12. Ronald F. Youngblood calls Hannah's hymn "the seedplot for Mary's Magnificat." See his comparison of the two songs in "1 & 2 Samuel," 579. W. H. B. Proby notes, "It is evident, then, on the most superficial examination of the song, that the song has a much wider reference than to the occasion which called it forth." The Song of Hannah "might truly be called the Old Testament *rehearsal*" of the Magnificat (p. 45; see especially his chart on p. 46). Proby also rightly comments, "Thus we may observe by the way, that while the language of the song is the language of the *Magnificat*, the utterance of it by Hannah after the birth of Samuel answers to the utterance of the *Benedictus* by Zacharias after the birth of John the Baptist. For Samuel was to David what John the Baptist was to Christ." *The Ten Canticles of the Old Testament Canon: Namely the Songs of Moses (First and Second), Deborah, Hannah, Isaiah (First, Second, and Third), Hezekiah, Jonah, and Habakkuk* (London: Rivingtons, 1874), 47.

than Solomon" (Luke 11:31). The people cry out, "Can this be the son of David?" (Matt. 12:23). The resounding answer is yes! This is "the Lion of the tribe of Judah, the Root of David" (Rev. 5:5). Yes! "Hosanna to the Son of David! . . . Hosanna in the highest!" (Matt. 21:9).

All this explains why Paul can write, "Remember Jesus Christ, raised from the dead, a descendant of David: such is my gospel" (2 Tim. 2:8, NAB). What's the gospel? What's the good news? Hannah is looking right at it! The good news is that Jesus is the King, the Anointed One. He is the one to whom God has given strength and power to judge the nations and to rescue the righteous.

## Steps to the Savior

At the end of the last chapter, I spoke of Scripture as a puzzle, and explained that putting all the pieces together forms the revelation of God in Christ. As I conclude this chapter, allow me to speak of *steps*. Perhaps the most fascinating discovery in my study of these scriptural songs is that of progression. Each scriptural song forms a step in a progression that leads to Jesus.

The apostle Paul, aware of this progression and its significance, walks his hearers up these steps in his sermon recorded in Acts 13:16–23—from Egypt to the wilderness to the judges to Christ:

> Men of Israel and you who fear God, listen. The God of this people Israel chose our fathers and made the people great during their stay in the land of Egypt, and with uplifted arm he led them out of it. And for about forty years he put up with them in the wilderness. And after destroying seven

nations in the land of Canaan, he gave them their land as an inheritance. All this took about 450 years. And after that he gave them judges until Samuel the prophet. Then they asked for a king, and God gave them Saul the son of Kish, a man of the tribe of Benjamin, for forty years. And when he had removed him, he raised up David to be their king, of whom he testified and said, "I have found in David the son of Jesse a man after my heart, who will do all my will." Of this man's offspring God has brought to Israel a Savior, Jesus, as he promised.

I don't know why you are a Christian, but what is summarized above is one of the reasons I'm one. I can't explain, except it be of God, how one book, written by so many different authors from so many different times, can come up with themes that perfectly intersect and connect in one person, with steps which all lead to one person.

I don't know if you have ever read the Qur'an, but it does nothing of the kind. Nor do any of the other so-called "holy" books. But with the Bible, it's a different story, for the Bible tells a story, a true and convincing story: The Christ is coming (that's the Old Testament); the Christ has come (that's the New Testament). It echoes and expands the two songs in Samuel, singing of salvation and of the Savior.

Unbelievers can write off our religious experiences, but I don't think they can so easily write off this. And that is why all of us, after we have looked at the way God worked, and the way he works, and the way he will work, ought to bow the knee and "kiss the Son" (Ps. 2:12), paying homage to Jesus, God's anointed King, who has come to save and will come to judge.

A prayer of Habakkuk the prophet, according to Shigionoth.
<sup>2</sup> O Lᴏʀᴅ, I have heard the report of you,
and your work, O Lᴏʀᴅ, do I fear.
In the midst of the years revive it;
in the midst of the years make it known;
in wrath remember mercy.
. . . . . . . . . . . . . . . . . . . . . . .
<sup>17</sup> Though the fig tree should not blossom,
nor fruit be on the vines,
the produce of the olive fail
and the fields yield no food,
the flock be cut off from the fold
and there be no herd in the stalls,
<sup>18</sup> yet I will rejoice in the Lᴏʀᴅ;
I will take joy in the God of my salvation.
<sup>19</sup> Gᴏᴅ, the Lord, is my strength;
he makes my feet like the deer's;
he makes me tread on my high places.
(Hab. 3:1–2, 17–19a)

# 5

# The Song of Habakkuk: A Time to Wait—for Wrath

IN HER CELEBRATED novel, *Uncle Tom's Cabin*, Harriet Beecher Stowe provides a dramatic depiction of the common cruelties of slavery in America. In perhaps the most theologically charged scene in this book, George and his wife Eliza, two runaway slaves, along with Simeon, an old, white Quaker who is assisting in their escape, learn that a party of slave traders and officers of the law are close at hand. So George in his anger, fear, and frustration thunders:

> Is God on their side? Does he see all they do? Why does he let such things happen? . . . They are rich, and healthy, and happy . . . expecting to go to heaven; and they get along so easy in the world, and have it all their own way; [while] poor, honest, faithful Christians—Christians . . . better than they—are lying in the very dust under their feet. They buy 'em and sell 'em, and make trade of their heart's blood, and groans and tears—and God *lets* them.[1]

1. Harriet Beecher Stowe, *Uncle Tom's Cabin*, Everyman's Library (repr., New York: Knopf, 1994), 216.

The book of Habakkuk begins with a similar thundering, with a poor, honest, faithful man of God crying out to his seemingly unfair and uncaring God. In the very first word of this book, the prophet says,

> O LORD, how long shall I cry for help,
>     and you will not hear?
> Or cry to you "Violence!"
>     and you will not save?
> Why do you make me see iniquity,
>     and why do you idly look at wrong? (1:2–3a)

With a striking similarity to the slavery situation of nineteenth-century America, the prophet Habakkuk in his day witnessed the self-professed "people of God" acting wickedly toward others who go by that same name. "The wicked surround the righteous," he complains to God. "Destruction and violence are before me; strife and contention arise," he says, while "the law is paralyzed" and "justice goes forth perverted" (vv. 3b–4).

## Three Movements

If we think of the book of Habakkuk as a symphony in three movements, with each of its chapters representing a movement, then the first two movements resound with the steady beat of crashing cymbals. The first crash comes in 1:2–4, where the prophet questions God: Why have you not judged Judah's wickedness? Why do the wicked within the people of God go unpunished? Where is your jealousy for your name and reputation? When will vengeance and vindication come?

The Lord, so it seems, answers almost immediately (1:5–11). God's plan for punishment has been decided and is now decreed. The Chaldeans are coming. The brutal Babylonians, with their skill and savagery, will discipline the disobedient.

With this, Habakkuk is taken aback. He recoils at the thought of this unholy alliance. And so the cymbals strike again. The prophet, honestly seeking to see the sense of the situation,[2] sounds forth (in 1:12–17), "How can you, O God, you who have purer eyes than to see evil and who cannot look at wrong, how can you discipline your people with a people whose sin is far greater?" Implicit in this question is another related question, "And what will become of the righteous remnant, including me?"

Chapter 2 takes up the Lord's twofold reply. First, God calms the prophet's fears. The righteous remnant will be preserved, for "those who humbly rely on me will live." Second and conversely, the proud, those who rely on their own strength, will die. Woe will come upon Babylon. What they have sown they will soon reap. Like a boomerang, all the evils that they have thrown upon the world will come back to strike them.[3]

Now, while the noise and the reverberation of these crashes are still in the air, the third and final movement begins (chapter 3) as the soft and sweet sound of submission comes from a soloist's voice. It is the prophet himself. He has put down his

---

2. William Sanford LaSor et al. point out: "Habakkuk's motive in posing these questions was neither idle curiosity nor a desire to dabble in divine affairs. He was an honest and devout seeker after truth." *Old Testament Survey: The Message, Form, and Background of the Old Testament* (Grand Rapids: Eerdmans, 1996), 324.

3. For an excellent summary of the book of Habakkuk, see ibid., 323–27.

cymbals, and now he sings.[4] He sings of his wholehearted trust in his sovereign and good God.[5]

## Faith Waits for Wrath

Musically, there are a number of ways to change the mood or atmosphere of a song. A brilliant example of this is found in Bach's "Crucifixus" from his Mass in B Minor. As the choir sings of Jesus' crucifixion under Pontus Pilate, there are thirteen (the unlucky or evil number) repetitions of the diabolical-sounding ground bass. This symbolizes the temporary triumph of evil. However, this evil is danced upon, if you will, by the harmony, which leads the hearers up and out from the pit, triumphing in the death of death in the death of Christ.[6]

Another example is that of the pipe organ. At College Church in Wheaton, where I once pastored, the organist sometimes used a change of registration to effect this change. I can remember specifically how our organist, H. E. Singley, did this with my version of the Song of Hannah, "Our King, God Does Exalt." During the final verse of that hymn, he changed registrations on the organ when we shifted from singing of the judgment of the wicked to singing of God's exaltation of his anointed. In this way he changed the feel from somberness to celebration.

4. For some of the many reasons why Habakkuk's prayer should be viewed also as a song, see Carl E. Armerding, "Obadiah, Nahum, Habakkuk," in *Expositor's Bible Commentary*, ed. Frank E. Gaebelein, vol. 7 (Grand Rapids: Zondervan, 1992), 520.

5. This is why the poet Michel Dayton named his remarkable poem on this text "A Song of the Faithful."

6. See Andrew Wilson-Dickson, *The Story of Christian Music* (Minneapolis: Fortress, 1992), 96.

A final way to produce an atmospheric shift musically is through a key change. For example, one can go from a lower key in the first three verses of a hymn to a higher key, usually a half step up, in the final verse.

Similarly, in verses 16–19—the climax of Habakkuk's hymn of faith and the "mountaintop" from which we will view the rest of the song—there is *poetically* a key change. Even more than that, what happens here (and rarely happens in music) is that Habakkuk, if you will allow me, moves from a minor key to a major key. He does this twice, each time when he strikes the word "yet." Look below and notice the changes.

> I hear, and my body trembles;
>> my lips quiver at the sound;
> rottenness enters into my bones;
>> my legs tremble beneath me.
> *Yet* I will quietly wait for the day of trouble
>> to come upon people who invade us.
> Though the fig tree should not blossom,
>> nor fruit be on the vines,
> the produce of the olive fail
>> and the fields yield no food,
> the flock be cut off from the fold
>> and there be no herd in the stalls,
> *yet* I will rejoice in the LORD;
>> I will take joy in the God of my salvation.
> GOD, the Lord, is my strength;
>> he makes my feet like the deer's;
>> he makes me tread on my high places. (Hab. 3:16–19)

I want us to hear these two major keys and then join in the singing.

# The First Major Key

The first major key of faith sounds like this: Faith waits for wrath. Remember, Habakkuk has been told that the cruel Chaldeans are coming, and he reacts in fear. "I hear [they're coming], and [so] my body trembles; my lips quiver at the sound; rottenness enters into my bones; my legs tremble beneath me" (v. 16a). Just as our Lord's thoughts of drinking the cup of God's wrath produced a sweat of blood at Gethsemane, so here Habakkuk's fear manifests itself physically, from head to toe, or from lips to legs.

But since he knows God's "work" of wrath in the past, as he states so clearly in verse 2 and then illustrates so thoroughly in verses 3–15, his trembling gives way to trust.[7] "Yet I will quietly wait for the day of trouble to come upon people [these Babylonians] who invade us" (v. 16b). He will wait quietly, without complaint. He will wait for God's wrath to fall upon this evil empire, just as it fell upon the Egyptians in the Song of Moses, upon the Canaanites in the Song of Deborah, and upon the enemies of David in the Song of Hannah.

Now I know that, as much as we would like to sing these major keys with Habakkuk during the minor moments of our lives, this first major key is quite unfamiliar to many of us. That is, when we think of faith, we are not likely to include *waiting for wrath*. There are at least two reasons for this.[8]

7. See Theodore Hiebert, "The Use of Inclusion in Habakkuk 3," in *Directions in Biblical Hebrew Poetry*, ed. Elaine R. Follis (Sheffield: JSOT Press, 1987), 280. Hiebert references Rudolf Otto's work on the *mysterium tremendum* in his important work, *The Idea of the Holy* (London: Oxford University Press, 1973), 31–40.

8. I have limited the scope of cognitive dissonances. Later I will argue against opinions like those of C. S. Lewis in his *Reflections on the Psalms*. Lewis thought that "waiting for wrath," as I've labeled it, is a hallmark of the oppressed throughout history, but that it is neither necessary nor virtuous as a characteristic of all believers at all times, especially now in the age of Christ.

First, we tend to have an ahistorical understanding of our faith. That is, our faith is based not so much upon God's work in the past as it is upon God's work in the present. If asked why we believe, we would probably say, "I believe in God because this or that is happening in my life here and now." Such faith is something we can see or at least sense.

Now certainly there is some truth to this. But it is interesting to note that the faith of the men and women of the Bible who sing the scriptural songs is historically grounded. For example, when Mary hears the news of her conception of Jesus, she first expresses her faith in the here and now: "Lord, I am so overwhelmed that you would choose me for such a task." (That's the sense of what she says.) But then her faith quickly moves from the present to the past. She speaks of Abraham: "Ah, Lord, but it is just as you promised our father Abraham" (cf. Luke 1:55). You see, her faith is not ahistorical. It's not a here-and-now only, existential "leap of faith"—with nothing assured beneath it.[9] Rather, her faith is based on a foundation of facts, on historical promises and their fulfillments.

Thus far in our study of the Songs of Scripture, this has been the pattern. Therefore, it should come as no surprise that this pattern emerges in Habakkuk's hymn. With splendid literary technique, the prophet, in verses 3–15, mixes many events of God's redemptive history, notably the exodus and the conquest, into one memory. In other words, he remembers God's "work"—his works of judgment in the past. And God's wrath in the past provides the prophet's foundation of faith in the present. He can live with his fears because he knows God is faithful to judge. The Lord is faithful and will be faithful because he was faithful. That's how Habakkuk reasons.

It is essential that we know our history—the history of God's work in the world, as recorded in his Word. The more

9. Contra Søren Kierkegaard's depiction of Mary in *Fear and Trembling*.

SERMONS ON THE SONGS

historically grounded our faith is, the more likely it is that we will trust God *and* that we will recognize that a component of our faith (like the faith of those of old) should be waiting for wrath.

The ahistorical understanding of our faith keeps us from reaching the heights, the high notes of Habakkuk's faith. Also keeping us down is our false notion that wrath is not righteous. We wouldn't say that God's judgments are not good, but some of us think that judgment itself is not good. The idea is that "negative" themes are always bad.

I say this because Christians today, more than ever, avoid speaking, writing, and certainly *singing* about this topic.[10] Let me give you an illustration of what I'm saying. Most churches today are registered with an organization called CCLI—Christian Copyright Licensing International.[11] This is a database that contains over 200,000 worship songs, including most contemporary choruses, but also many of the classic evangelical hymns from Watts, Wesley, Doddridge, Newton, Cowper, Crosby, and the like. Formerly, this Internet database had a tab which listed 125 song themes. Today it lists only the top ten themes, the most popular of which is "acceptance." In the older Internet edition, only one of the 125 themes listed was negative, and that was the theme of "judgment." And in this category there were only seven songs. Of those seven songs, one of them was entitled "Oh Buddha" (I'm not kidding.) The third verse of this song goes:

Well, ol' Buddha was a man, and I'm sure that he meant well.
But I pray for his disciples lest they wind up in Hell.
And I am sure that ol' Mohammed thought he knew the way.

10. See chapter 9.
11. See www.ccli.com.

94

But it won't be Hare Krishna we stand before on the Judgment Day.[12]

Profound, isn't it? C. S. Lewis once called the Christian hymnody of his day "fifth-rate poems set to sixth-rate music."[13] I wonder what he'd call this?

In addition to reviewing the lyrics of the so-called "judgment" songs a few years ago, I recently searched CCLI's new and updated database for certain words and the number of songs in which they appear.[14] When I typed in the word "wrath," I discovered that there were 425 songs that contained that word.[15] When I typed in "judgment," I found 570 songs; "anger" produced 624.

That may sound balanced until you remember there are over 200,000 songs in this database. Much more common were these words: "laugh," in 1,041 songs; "happy," in 2,246; "heart," in 35,746; "love," in 36,171; and "me," in 37,258. The word "football" is in 25 songs, "yell" in 77, "hug" in 150, "mama" in 160, "dog" in 188, "drums" in 261, "toes" in 262, "car" in 274, "hair" in 406, "crazy" in 408, "jump" in 514, "wild" in 525, "fun" in 529, "ain't" in 729, "girl" in 863, "clap" in 943, "drunk" in 1,722, "dance" in 3,170, "gonna" in 3,562, "heal" in 6,737, and "feel" in 9,571. Then we have phrases like "feeling your touch" in 144, "touch me" in 482, "hold me" in 1,652, "love me" in 3,283, and "my heart" in 16,267. So, you tell me. Is there a problem with Christian music when we have only 425

12. Mark Farrow, CCLI 34116.

13. C. S. Lewis, *God in the Dock: Essays on Theology and Ethics* (Grand Rapids: Eerdmans, 1970), 61–62.

14. I searched www.ccli.com/LicenseHolder/Search/SongSearch.aspx on March 24, 2009.

15. It should be noted that some songs were listed a few times. For example, Charles Wesley's "Depth of Mercy" and Julie Ward Howe's "Battle Hymn of the Republic" were both listed ten times (due to remakes or "covers").

songs that contain the word "wrath" and more than eight times as many songs containing "gonna"?

To give you a biblical perspective on some of these words, in the English Standard Version of the Bible the word "wrath" appears 212 times and the word "love" 550 times (do you see the balance there?), but the word "laugh" appears only 17 times and "happy" 11 times. In the book of Psalms, the word "wrath" appears 26 times, the word "love" appears 151 times, the word "laugh" or "laughter" appears 4 times, and the word "happy" sadly does not appear at all.

Now, I know that such word searches do not provide a completely accurate assessment. Just because the word "you" appears 8,333 times in the Bible and the word "God" appears only 3,810 times, we cannot conclude that the Bible is mostly about "you." Yet I do think this data establishes that most Christians (especially in the first decade of the twenty-first century) have stopped singing about God's righteous triumphs, his judgments of the wicked.[16]

But why? It is certainly not because the Old Testament provides a different model. Hasn't it been striking to you how much the Songs of Scripture sing of judgment? It has been to me. Just look at the song before us now. Look at Habakkuk 3:2, "In wrath remember mercy." Why doesn't it just say, "Be merciful"? That's how we would say it, wouldn't we? We'd leave out the reference to wrath and be quite content with ourselves. Or look at verses 5, 8, 9, and 12. Verse 12 says, "You marched through the earth in fury; you threshed the nations in anger." Or look at verses 14 and 15. It's everywhere here, isn't it?

"Well," you might say, "that's just the problem. We are only looking in the Old Testament; the New Testament knows noth-

---

16. Recently I read through the hymnal used at College Church in Wheaton, *Hymns for the Living Church* (Carol Stream, IL: Hope, 1974). This is a typical hymnal used in the church during the last generation. I found only three songs in it that address the themes of wrath and judgment. For more on this, see chapter 9.

ing of this." That is a common misconception. For while it is true that our Lord Jesus demonstrated mercy ("Father, forgive them, for they know not what they are doing") and taught mercy ("Love your enemies"), that mercy does not nullify what the Gospels and Epistles also teach on the theme of waiting for wrath. The theme of judgment is common enough in the New Testament (2 Peter and Jude should suffice to make that point). But so too is the theme of joy over judgment. For example, 2 Thessalonians 1:6–10 says:

> Since indeed God considers it just to repay with affliction those who afflict you, and to grant relief to you who are afflicted as well as to us, when the Lord Jesus is revealed from heaven with his mighty angels in flaming fire, inflicting vengeance on those who do not know God and on those who do not obey the gospel of our Lord Jesus. They will suffer the punishment of eternal destruction, away from the presence of the Lord and from the glory of his might, when he comes on that day to be glorified in his saints, and to be marveled at among all who have believed, because our testimony to you was believed.

The reference to Christ being "glorified in his saints" and being "marveled at among all who have believed" when the wicked "suffer the punishment of eternal destruction" expresses joy in judgment or at least praise in judgment.

The same theme is common in the book of Revelation, especially in its prayers and songs. For example, in the Song of the Lamb the saints sing to Jesus, "Worthy are you to take the scroll and to open its seals" (Rev. 5:9). These seven seals are the seven coming judgments. And in Revelation 11:17 we hear, "We give thanks to you, Lord God Almighty, who is and who was, for you have taken your great power and begun to reign. The nations raged, but your wrath came." In 12:7–12 the heavens are called to "rejoice" because of the defeat of Satan and his angels. In 15:1ff. the Song of Moses becomes the praise song of heaven. In 16:5 we hear, "Just are you, O Holy One, who is and who was, for you brought these judgments." Chapters 18–19 show us God's judgment falling upon what John calls "Babylon"—a new and final Babylon—and we hear in 18:2, "Fallen, fallen is Babylon the great!" And 18:10 says, "Alas! Alas! You great city, you mighty city, Babylon! For in a single hour your judgment has come." Finally, in 19:1–2 we hear heaven's hallelujah chorus: "Hallelujah! Salvation and glory and power belong to our God, for his judgments are true and just."

You see, the Bible from top to tail sings of salvation, which includes rescue and wrath. Yet we don't sing like the Bible sings—like Habakkuk did of waiting for wrath—because of our notion that wrath is not righteous, that judgment is not good. That notion is false because the Bible teaches that the wrath of God is righteous.

I was especially stuck by this reality when I came across a book written by Isaac Watts, the great hymn writer of the eighteenth century.[17] The book is entitled *Divine and Moral Songs for the Use of Children*.[18] This book is full of children's songs that talk about, among other things, the wrath of God. One example comes from the song "Solemn Thoughts on God and Death."[19] (How's that for a title for a children's song?) The first verse goes like this:

17. Or even better, we can call Watts "the great liberator of hymnody in English," as Erik Routley does. See Paul A. Richardson, ed., *A Panorama of Christian Hymnody* (Chicago: GIA Publications, 2005), 39.

18. Isaac Watts, *Divine and Moral Songs for the Use of Children* (repr., Whitefish, MT: Kessinger Publishing, 2003), 25, 91.

19. Cf. Charles Wesley, "Terrible Thought, Shall I Alone," in *Hymns for Children* (1763). For some interesting and wonderful thoughts on what children should sing, see Carl Schalk's chapter, "Ambrose, the Children, and Advent," in *First Person Singular: Reflections on Worship, Liturgy, and Children* (St. Louis: MorningStar, 1998), 17–19. Schalk discusses what the children of Ambrose's church likely sang. He writes, "What did the children sing? Most likely some hymns of Ambrose, those wonderfully rich and sturdy hymns, a few of which are still found in today's hymnals. The children might have been singing some words they didn't quite understand; the melodies might even have been in those 'minor keys.' But they sang along with all the faithful, their young

There is a God that reigns above
Lord of the heavens, and earth, and seas
I fear his wrath, I ask his love
And with my lips I sing his praise.

Another example comes from the twelfth verse of Watts' "Cradle Hymn." After we have sung of the incarnation, we sing,

'Twas to save thee, child, from dying,
Save my dear from burning flame,
Bitter groans and endless crying,
That thy blest Redeemer came.

Those lyrics may be compared with those of one of our most popular children's songs—"Children of the Lord" or "The Arky, Arky Song."[20] Promisingly, the song's theme is the Genesis flood that God sent as a judgment upon the world. Yet look at these lyrics and see if you notice any hint of judgment:

God told Noah there's going to be a floody, floody,
God told Noah there's going to be a floody, floody,
Get those animals out of the muddy, muddy,
Children of the Lord.

God told Noah to build him an arky, arky,
God told Noah to build him an arky, arky,

---

faith shaped, molded, and nurtured by their song" (p. 17). Jerome, another church father, believed that psalm singing should be such a part of a child's upbringing that "a little girl should know the Psalter by heart by the age of seven." Quoted in Johannes Quasten, *Music and Worship in Pagan and Christian Antiquity*, trans. Boniface Ramsey (Washington: National Association of Pastoral Musicians, 1983), 138.

20. This song would be a good example of Elsie H. Sprigg's comment on children's songs: "There is a modern tendency to present God as what may be described as a celestial zoo man or an omnipotent St. Francis." Quoted in Schalk, *First Person Singular*, 17–18.

Build it out of gopher barky, barky,
Children of the Lord.

The animals, they came in, they came in by twosies,
      twosies,
The animals, they came in, they came in by twosies,
      twosies,
Elephants and kangaroosies, roosies,
Children of the Lord.

It rained, it rained for forty nights and daysies, daysies,
It rained, it rained for forty nights and daysies, daysies,
Almost drove poor Noah crazy, crazy,
Children of the Lord.

The sun came out and dried up the landy, landy,
The sun came out and dried up the landy, landy,
Everything was fine and dandy, dandy,
Children of the Lord.

This is the end of, the end of our story, story,
This is the end of, the end of our story, story,
Everything was hunky dory, dory,
Children of the Lord.

We all know how fun this song is to sing. And it does have some real educational value to it—learning about complex rhyme schemes and what have you (I'm kidding). There is only one thing missing, however, from the story, story. What's missing? Well, the wrath of God is missing! And if you take the wrath out of that story, you take out the deliverance. If you take out the wrath, you take out the mercy. If you take out the wrath, you take out the love.

Everything was not hunky dory for those who did not enter the ark in faith. And everything will not be hunky dory for those who do not trust in Christ. Jesus saves us from something. He saves us from "the wrath to come" (1 Thess. 1:10).

## You Are What You Sing

We all know the truth of the slogan, "You are what you eat." That is, if you eat fatty foods, you get fat. But few of us realize also that "you are what you sing."[21] That is, if you sing only fluffy songs, your theology and doxology—the way you view and worship God—becomes fatty and fluffy.

I have heard it said that the Methodist movement of the eighteenth century never needed its own book of systematic theology (like so many other movements) because it had the hymns of Charles Wesley. Now there's some truth to that! What we sing is often how we think about God. And, sadly, if we used just the top songs sung in evangelical churches today—both choruses and hymns—to write our systematic theology, there would be volumes and volumes on God's love and only a pamphlet on God's wrath. With Habakkuk, however ("in your wrath remember mercy"), there are two full volumes, one on wrath and one on mercy.

21. Here are two good quotes on this theme: "We are our hymns; they inform our faith, and are invariably written from a standpoint of faith. It is sometimes said in liturgical circles, 'Lex credenda, lex orandi,' which means 'What they pray, they believe,' implying that whatever we say in formal prayers, we end up believing." Gordon Giles, *The Music of Praise: Meditations on Great Hymns of the Church* (Peabody, MA: Hendrickson, 2004), 9. "When faced with a complaining parishioner who wanted to know why the congregation was not allowed a particular kind of music in worship, the late Dr. Erik Routley simply replied, 'You can't have it because it is not good for you.'" Quoted in Calvin M. Johansson, *Discipling Music Ministry: Twenty-first Century Directions* (Peabody, MA: Hendrickson, 1992), 168.

# Faith Rejoices in God, Even in Adversity

So the first major key of faith (major, not minor!) is that faith waits for wrath. Now, the second major key is that faith rejoices in God, even in adversity. Look with me at verses 17–19. Oh, these are beautiful verses! Here Habakkuk sings,

> Though the fig tree should not blossom,
>     nor fruit be on the vines,
> the produce of the olive fail
>     and the fields yield no food,
> the flock be cut off from the fold
>     and there be no herd in the stalls,
> yet I will rejoice in the LORD;
>     I will take joy in the God of my salvation.
> GOD, the Lord, is my strength;
>     he makes my feet like the deer's;
>     he makes me tread on my high places.

In 2:4, the Lord tells the prophet, "The righteous shall live by his faith" (which is quoted three times in the New Testament).[22] Here, before our very eyes, that message finds its fulfillment,[23] or better, its embodiment. Here Habakkuk, the righteous man, lives! He lives by faith, by "his steadfast trust" in God.[24]

22. See Rom. 1:17; Gal. 3:11; Heb. 10:38ff. LaSor notes, "This principle became the seed plot for Paul's key doctrine of justification by faith. . . . What Habakkuk learned to be God's principle of operation in the Babylonian invasion, Paul with inspired insight saw to be God's universal principle of salvation." *Old Testament Survey*, 327. John Calvin summarizes, "We indeed know that God cannot be rightly and from the heart worshipped but in faith." John Owen, trans., *Commentaries on the Minor Prophets*, Calvin's Commentaries (repr., Grand Rapids: Baker, 1993), 15:132.

23. O. Palmer Robertson, *The Books of Nahum, Habakkuk, and Zephaniah*, NICOT (Grand Rapids: Eerdmans, 1994), 247.

24. Ibid., 246.

We sometimes say or hear others say, "I never could have made it through that without my faith." Well, the prophet would say, more precisely, "I never could have made it through that without my God"[25]—"GOD, the Lord, is my strength; *he* makes my feet like the deer's; *he* makes me tread on my high places."

Here, as Habakkuk acknowledges the effects of Israel's apostasy (that is, a devastated economy, which will come from a desolate land, which will come from "the ravages of war"),[26] he also acknowledges his ultimate allegiance. There will be no food. There will be no money. But that matters not, for God alone is his sustenance, and God alone his treasure. Habakkuk was like Job, on the ash heap, who could lift his heavy heart to heaven and say, "I know that my Redeemer lives" (Job 19:25).[27] The man of faith trusts God—no matter what.

## How Does Your Faith Fare?

The Word of God (in a very gracious and inviting way) places before our eyes extreme examples of persevering faith—whether it is Job or Habakkuk or David or Jeremiah or Peter or Paul. It holds up these heroes of faith as lights for us to follow in the dark nights of our souls.

So how well do you follow? How does your faith fare? That's the question this song sings to us. Do you have a faith like Habakkuk's—a faith that rejoices in God, even in adversity? Do you have

25. This insight is from a personal conversation with Michael Graves, associate professor of Old Testament at Wheaton College.

26. Robertson, *The Books of Nahum, Habakkuk, and Zephaniah*, 243.

27. Habakkuk was also like Isaiah, for, as C. F. Keil notes, "Here it is a figurative expression for the fresh and joyous strength acquired in God, which Isaiah calls rising up with eagles' wings (Isa. 40:29–31)." See C. F. Keil and F. Delitzsch, *Commentary on the Old Testament* (repr., Peabody, MA: Hendrickson, 2006), 10:428.

a faith that can endure the crosses of this world because of the joy set before you? Is your faith such that, when all is slippery around you and the weight of this world is pulling you down into the deepest valley, you can stand surefooted, like a resilient, graceful, steady, untiring deer? Do you have a faith like that?

"Well," you might say, "to be honest, no . . . or not always. I don't always live by faith through times of adversity." You might even go on to admit, "I have a hard time trusting God even when the little things go wrong—a bad day or a bad date or even a bad haircut. Even these little things trip up my trust. I can't imagine how I'd respond if I knew the Babylonians were coming to town." Well, if this is how you feel, let me encourage you with the Word of God to walk not by sight, but by faith, which is, as Hebrews 11:1 summarizes, "the conviction of things not seen."

Two encouragements to live by faith come from 1 Peter 4:12–13. Here Peter writes, "Beloved, do not be surprised at the fiery trial when it comes upon you to test you [i.e., to test the genuineness of your faith], as though something strange were happening to you" (v. 12). So, first, don't be surprised by suffering. We have a tough time enduring hardship because we think that hardships are strange or abnormal. "No," Peter says, "they are quite normal. Expect them." Peter goes on to give a second word of encouragement: "But rejoice insofar as you share Christ's sufferings, that you may also rejoice and be glad when his glory is revealed" (v. 13). Don't be surprised by suffering; in fact, see suffering as an opportunity for blessing—not only future blessing, but also present blessing, sharing now in the sufferings of Christ, so as to be more like him. The more suffering (this kind of suffering), the more sanctification; the more pain, the more possibility for purification—think of it that way.

Another way in which Scripture encourages us to walk by faith is by having a renewed vision of God. In Hebrews 11, the heroes of faith are paraded before us, one after another, to encourage us to keep going and to keep believing. This parade culminates in Hebrews 12:2, where we are told to persevere, "looking to Jesus, the founder and perfecter of our faith." The best way to be encouraged to walk by faith is to have a vision of God and a vision of his beloved Son.[28]

In the Sacred Museum of the Vatican, there is a sixteenth-century sculpture by Gian Lorenzo Bernini entitled *Habakkuk and the Angel*. In this masterpiece, Habakkuk is holding a packed bag, as if he is traveling somewhere, and his movement is forward, as if he is walking ahead. However, his movement is impeded by an angel hovering above him, who has grabbed this startled prophet by the hair, as if lifting him to heaven. There is something about that image that is so apropos to us. Some of us are very much on our own way, walking in a very different direction than God would have us walk. We need to be redirected, to be pulled by the hair, if you will, up into the heavens to see what Habakkuk saw (1:1)—a vision of God. For only a vision of the triune God can produce this kind of faith, this living, walking, moving forward, lifted high, trust-in-God-even-in-adversity kind of faith.

## "He Will Make All Right Hereafter"

In *Uncle Tom's Cabin*, after George complains about God— "Is God on their side?"—Simeon, a courageous Christian who daily risks his life for slaves, opens his Bible and reads the first eleven verses of Psalm 73, where the psalmist confesses his envy

---

28. Habakkuk moves from complaint to consecration, for he has seen God (Hab. 1:1), as did Job: "I had heard of you by the hearing of the ear, but now my eye sees you" (Job 42:5).

of the arrogant, his problem with the prosperity of the wicked. "Why do they get away with it?" is the psalmist's basic question. At this point, Simeon pauses, turns to George, and asks, "George, is not that the way you feel?" To that he replies, "It is so, indeed, as well as I could have written it myself."[29]

Then Simeon continues, reading how the psalmist comes into the sanctuary of God, where he sees God rightly. There he has a vision of God's wrath coming upon all wrongdoers and a vision of God's compassion showering his saints, loving the lowly. "It is good for me," the psalmist says, "to draw near unto God. I have put my trust in the Lord" (cf. v. 28).

These words "breathed by the friendly old man," we are told, "stole like sacred music over the harassed and chafed spirit of George." And Simeon said to him,

> George, if this world were all . . . you might, indeed, ask, "where is the Lord?" But it is often those who have least of all in this life whom he chooseth for the kingdom. Put thy trust in him and, no matter what befalls you here, he will make all right hereafter.[30]

"Put thy trust in him and, no matter what befalls you here, he will make all right hereafter"—that is the message of the book and of the Song of Habakkuk! God *will* make everything right. He will judge the wicked within the church, and he will judge the wicked within the world. No matter what befalls you—famine, affliction, persecution, sickness, poverty—put your trust in him!

29. Stowe, *Uncle Tom's Cabin*, 216–17.
30. Ibid., 217.

# PART TWO

# Applications for Christian Worship

And they sang a new song, saying,
"Worthy are you to take the scroll
    and to open its seals,
for you were slain, and by your blood you ransomed people
        for God
    from every tribe and language and people and nation,
[10] and you have made them a kingdom and priests to our
        God,
    and they shall reign on the earth."
            . . .

"To him who sits on the throne and to the Lamb be blessing
and honor and glory and might forever and ever!" (Rev. 5:9–10,
13b)

# 6

# Come, Christians, Join to Sing!

IN HIS *Homily on Psalm 42*, John Chrysostom begins his treatment of the familiar first verse—"As a deer pants for flowing streams, so pants my soul for you, O God"—with these words:

> Nothing, in fact, nothing so uplifts the soul, gives it wings, liberates it from the earth, looses the shackles of the body, promotes its values and its scorn for everything in this world as harmonious music and a divine song rhythmically composed.[1]

In this sermon, the church father explains why this "piece of inspired composition in particular is recited to music."[2] His answer is twofold.

---

1. John Chrysostom, *Old Testament Homilies*, trans. Robert Charles Hill (Brookline, MA: Holy Cross Orthodox Press, 2003), 3:69.
   2. Ibid.

First, God uses music to make "the knowledge of spiritual things" (i.e., the lyrics of the Psalms) more desirable.[3] Just as a fussing baby is soothed by a nurse's lullaby or beasts of burden are pacified by the wayfarer's tune, so God's Word, when set to music, "lightens the load" of carrying its spiritual truths into our hearts.[4]

Second, God gave us his own songs as an edifying option. As opposed to "profane" and "lascivious songs," which upset "everything" and allow demons to "congregate," spiritual melodies allow the Spirit to attend and to sanctify.[5] Chrysostom explains:

> From profane songs, you see, harm and damage and many dire consequences would be introduced; the more intemperate and lawless of these songs lodge in the parts of the soul, and render it weaker and more remiss. From the psalms, by contrast, being spiritual, there comes great benefit, great advantage and much sanctification, and the basis for every value would be provided, since the words purify the soul and the Holy Spirit quickly alights on the soul singing such things.[6]

While we can debate the legitimacy of Chrysostom's critique of secular songs and the verity of his philosophical worldview, his conviction that the Word of God set to music is indeed a means by which, as he puts it, "the Holy Spirit quickly alights on the soul," is, broadly speaking, what I've sought to explore and teach. And his admonition to the church to sing "divine" songs, as he

3. Ibid.

4. Ibid., 69–70.

5. Ibid., 70. Similarly, John Calvin, in his preface to the *Geneva Psalter*, uses strong language for the "secular" songs of his times. He calls them "dishonest and shameless." Quoted in Calvin R. Stapert, *A New Song for an Old World: Musical Thought in the Early Church* (Grand Rapids: Eerdmans, 2007), 195.

6. John Chrysostom, *Old Testament Homilies*, 70.

calls them—a song which is taken from God's Word—is, narrowly speaking, what this entire book is a call to do.

## *Sola Scriptura* and the Six Songs

As I have studied the history of Christian music, I have been saddened that the six divine songs we have considered, which were apparently sung in the early church,[7] have been discarded by the contemporary church. They are in particular ignored by those churches within Christendom which claim *sola Scriptura* as a theological distinctive.[8] Why there are so few songs within the Protestant musical tradition based on the songs of Moses, Deborah, Hannah, and Habakkuk is an embarrassing mystery and irony.[9]

7. Adolf von Harnack writes, "Eusebius incidentally informs us that Christian children began by learning the canticles of the Bible." J. R. Wilkinson, trans., *Bible Reading in the Early Church* (repr., Eugene, OR: Wipf & Stock, 2005), 84. In this quotation, Harnack references the early church historian's *Preparation for the Gospel*, a book written, in Johannes Quasten's words, "to refute pagan polytheism and show the superiority of the Jewish religion, which served as a 'preparation for the gospel.'" *Patrology* (Allen, TX: Christian Classics, 1983), 3:329. After highlighting what Plato has to say about music, Eusebius concludes, "With good reason then among us also the children are trained to practice the songs made by divine prophets and hymns addressed to God" (12:20). So, assuming that the reference to "divine prophets" includes Moses and David at the very least, and perhaps also Habakkuk, Eusebius provides us with some evidence that children (and presumably adults) sang Old Testament songs.

8. In the Roman Catholic and Eastern Orthodox liturgies, these songs find their place. Both the Sarum Rite and the Roman Breviary of the Catholic Church contain most of the scriptural songs, and on occasion they are still sung in certain churches. The *kanones* of the Eastern church, the most complex of the Byzantine hymns, are based on the songs in these passages (in the LXX, including deuterocanonical sections): Ex. 15:1–19; Deut. 32:1–43; 1 Sam. 2:1–10; Isa. 26:9–19; Dan. 3:26–45, 52–56; Dan. 3:57–88; Jonah 2:3–10; Hab. 3:2–19; Luke 1:46–55; Luke 1:68–79. So Andrew Wilson-Dickson, *The Story of Christian Music* (Minneapolis: Fortress, 1992), 152. To my knowledge, these are still sung regularly.

9. The first English hymnbook that was not entirely based on the Psalms, *The Hymnes and Songs of the Church* (1623), contains ninety songs, thirty-two from Old

This book is an effort to solve this mystery, if you will, and to erase, in a small way, this irony. While it might be right to call it an effort to return to the singing of the earliest Christian communities

---

Testament texts (including Ex. 15, Deut. 32, Judg. 5, 1 Sam. 2, and Hab. 3). But it appears from later hymnals and writings that the scriptural songs were often disregarded. W. H. Proby laments this in *The Ten Canticles of the Old Testament Canon: Namely the Songs of Moses, Deborah, Hannah, Isaiah, Hezekiah, Jonah, and Habakkuk* (London: Rivingtons, 1874), which seeks to revive their use in the Anglican liturgy. In his preface he writes of the songs, "That their resumption would enrich our formularies to a great extent is, we suppose, unquestionable." I have concluded—after examining many post-1900 hymnals—that the "unquestionable enrichment" Proby hoped for is still to be hoped for.

Judging by the CCLI database, other online databases, and hymnals and songbooks in print, it would appear that Protestant churches today rarely, if ever, sing a song based directly on these Old Testament texts. In searching through www.nethymnal.org, with 10,000 hymns in its database, and the marvelous database www.hymnary.org, I found only two songs on these six texts—"Song of Hannah" (1 Sam. 2:1–10), by Emily R. Brink, and "Though the Fig Tree Shall Not Blossom" (Hab. 3), by Ernest Thompson (which draws upon biblical language and themes, but does not completely walk us through the text). I also found three more songs that reference a verse or a few verses from one of the six songs—"I Will Sing to the Lord" (Ex. 15:1–2), by Emily R. Brink; "Praise to God" (Ex. 15:1–2), by Anon.; "Great Is the Lord Almighty!" (Ex. 15:3–4), by Dennis L. Jernigan; "Give Ear, O Earth, Attend My Songs" (Deut. 32:1, 3–4, 34–38), by Calvin Seerveld; "Canta¡ Débora, Canta!" (Judg. 5:7, 31), by Luiza Cruz; "Sometimes a Light Surprises" (Hab. 3:17–18), by William Cowper; and possibly (I was unable to secure the lyrics) "Sing to the Lord, Who Has Vanquished the Horse and the Warrior," by Carl P. Daw Jr., and "Song of the Sea," by Niamh O'Kelly-Fischer (both based on Ex. 15). Beyond these online resources, as well as the twelve hymnals I read through, I found "O God, from Age to Age the Same" (on Hab. 3), by Timothy Dudley-Smith, and these songs by Christopher M. Idle: "I Will Sing the Lord's High Triumph" (Ex. 15), "Attend, All Heaven and Earth" (Deut. 32), and "In God the Lord My Heart Is Strong" and "My Heart Rejoices" (both on 1 Sam. 2:1–10). In an e-mail correspondence with Emily R. Brink, senior research fellow of the Calvin Institute of Christian Worship and program chair of the Calvin Symposium on Worship (and author of two of the hymns mentioned above), I was told, "I agree with your assessment, that OT texts, including the Psalms, have been neglected in Christian worship." From an e-mail received on May 21, 2009.

I have not counted songs that touch on (in one line) the crossing of the Red Sea, such as the famous John of Damascus text, "Come, Ye Faithful, Raise the Strain," or songs that summarize a theme—e.g., the reversal of fortune—such as "The Canticle of the Turning" (an excellent song based on the songs of Hannah and Mary).

or the earliest English hymnody,[10] it is more and simply an effort to return to the Word of God in the worship of God, to preserve the scriptural songs, as Luther would put it of the Psalms, "in the ears of the church."[11] The idea is not to preserve them "in a glass jar," as Peter Enns says of Exodus 15, "for future generations to gawk at," but rather to apply them as "models for worship," as songs that were written down for "those who live in the light of the resurrection of God's son" to ponder, study, and sing.[12]

The following chapters offer a way forward: a corrective and a call for the contemporary church.

## The Four Themes of the Six Songs

There are four themes in each of these six scriptural songs:

1. The Lord is at the center; that is, our God is addressed, adored, and "enlarged."
2. His mighty acts in salvation history are recounted.
3. His acts of judgment are rejoiced in.
4. His ways of living (practical wisdom)[13] are encouraged.

In the next four chapters, I will illustrate how the six scriptural songs sing of these themes. Then I will compare these themes (my "control," if you will) with the most popular contemporary Christian choruses (CCC),[14] as well as the most popular classic hymns

10. On the earliest English hymnody, see footnote 9.

11. Wilson-Dickson, *The Story of Christian Music*, 61.

12. Peter Enns, *Exodus*, NIVAC (Grand Rapids: Zondervan, 2000), 314.

13. Or "instruction in wise behavior" (Prov. 1:3, NASB).

14. See the appendix for a full listing of songs. I use the term "chorus" broadly to encompass any newer song, even if that song has a more traditional hymn structure, as does "In Christ Alone," for example.

(CH) sung in today's churches. The purpose of this is to show some strengths and weaknesses of our favorite lyrics, and to suggest compensating for those weaknesses by using the six scriptural songs.

In order to determine the top choruses, I used the CCLI database, which records what each individual church sings each Sunday. While this is not a perfect source (as churches can and do fail to record everything they sing), it is the most accurate source available.[15] This database lists the top twenty-five songs sung per six-month period. I gathered the names and lyrics of the top twenty-five songs sung in each six-month period from 2000 to 2008, and then determined the fifty songs that were the most popular during those years.[16]

I also determined the top twenty-five CH. Without a database comparable to that of the CCLI, this was more difficult, but in the end my list was no less "scientific."[17] To make this selection, I answered three questions:

1.  What lyrics[18] were written before 1800 (even if they first appeared in an English hymnal after 1800)?[19]

15. Chuck King, pastor of worship and music at College Church in Wheaton, told me in an e-mail of March 18, 2009, that the CCLI is "the *sine qua non* of P&W [praise and worship] trackage."
16. If I have counted correctly, there have been only sixty-one songs in the top twenty-five for any year from 2000 to 2008. Those other than the top fifty songs (other than the three hymn remakes) would further validate my findings.
17. Due to the difficulty of assembling the list, I decided to select only twenty-five hymns, instead of fifty. However, I have read through thousands of hymns, and have a good overall understanding of the content of pre-1800 hymns. I know which ones not on my list are still most often sung, notably "Sing Praise to God Who Reigns Above," "Jesus, the Very Thought of Thee," "There Is a Fountain," "Glorious Things of Thee Are Spoken," and "Be Still, My Soul!"
18. Here I do focus on the age of the lyrics, even if they were not translated into English until after 1800.
19. I realize that post-1800 hymns like "Holy, Holy, Holy," "Blessed Assurance, Jesus Is Mine," "Crown Him with Many Crowns," "Great Is Thy Faithfulness," "How Great Thou Art," "I Love Thy Kingdom, Lord," "Jesus Paid It All," "O the Deep, Deep

2. Of those "classics," which ones are still found in most contemporary American hymnals, especially the best-selling ones?[20]

3. Of those hymns, which ones are most often sung today?

---

Love of Jesus," "Joyful, Joyful, We Adore Thee," "Just As I Am," "Nearer My God to Thee," "When Peace like a River," and "Silent Night! Holy Night!" can and often are classified as "classic." Yet, both for the sake of clarity (a "classic" should be at least 200 years old) and for ease of selection (it would be more difficult to select the top twenty-five hymns if I added an additional 100 or 150 years), I have narrowed our focus to pre-1800 hymns. However, I have used some of the hymns just mentioned as examples to illustrate my points. In other words, I am well aware of their existence and their lyrical content. And if the most popular hymns from the later period were added to this study, the results of it would not change dramatically.

20. The database hymnary.org includes twenty-seven hymnals from many Protestant denominations and churches, including Southern Baptist, Christian Reformed, Anglican, Congregational, Lutheran, Episcopal, Church of God, Presbyterian, Reformed Church in America, Moravian, United Methodist, and Roman Catholic hymnals. It also lists a few other extensive databases (e.g., Christian Classic Ethereal Hymnary), a choral collection, and small classic collections (e.g., Watts, *Divine and Moral Songs*). In total, it is up to fifty books. The songs I selected as the CH were found in most of the twenty-seven hymnals. "And Can It Be That I Should Gain?" received the lowest score (in only eleven books), and "All Hail the Power of Jesus' Name" the highest (in forty-two books). The other songs scored between 16 and 33, the average being 23.48. This confirmed my selection.

"American Protestant Hymns Project: A Ranked List of Most Frequently Printed Hymns, 1737–1960," which is a recent scholarly study by Stephen A. Marini, confirmed my independent study and selection. Seventeen of the twenty-five hymns on my list were on that list, and those included on my list are only slightly debatable, since my project focuses not on what has been printed most often in America during the last two centuries, but rather on what is most popular now. So, while "A Mighty Fortress" and "And Can It Be?" are not found on the Marini list, they are, nevertheless, far more popular today than "I Am a Soldier of the Cross" (#5 on the Marini list) and "On Jordan's Stormy Banks" (#8). The two most debatable hymns on my list are "The God of Abraham Praise" and "Praise to the Lord, the Almighty." I selected the former because I already had a number of Watts's hymns on my list, as well as representative Christmas carols. I included the latter hymn because it has gained popularity through Fernando Ortega and other contemporary musicians. I selected it over "Blest Be the Tie" because that song is not often sung today. For the Marini list, see appendix I in Richard J. Mouw and Mark A. Noll, eds., *Wonderful Words of Life: Hymns in American Protestant History and Theology* (Grand Rapids: Eerdmans, 2004).

The last criterion, I'll admit, was based on my personal estimations and experience, in consultation with a few experts in the field.[21] Like my selection of the top choruses, my selection of the top hymns is somewhat imprecise, but not so imprecise as to affect my conclusions. In other words, if I used the two hundred hymns now most commonly sung,[22] the results would differ only slightly.[23]

To be clear, I am not, in this part of the book, comparing the four themes with all the hymns written before 1800 and all the choruses written after 1970. Such a study would be beyond my scope. I am merely looking at the songs that are most often sung today—whether the CH or the CCC—to see how well their lyrics compare with the six scriptural songs of our study. So, as we now move forward, our three basic questions are: (1) What themes are found in the scriptural songs? (2) Are these themes found in the songs most often sung in today's American churches?[24] (3) If they are not, what can we do to change that?

21. Besides comparing my list with hymnary.org and the Marini list, I discussed my selections with Chuck King and H. E. Singley. We were not in perfect agreement on the top twenty-five hymns, but none of my selections raised "red flags" for these experts.

22. I am not dealing with all of the original lyrics of the CH, but with the lyrics that are usually printed in today's hymnals. A Charles Wesley hymn, for example, may have originally had ten verses, but we commonly sing only four. It is those four which we will study. In other words, this is a study of recent (mostly post-1970s) English hymnals and choruses.

23. Before I finalized my list of the top twenty-five CH, I ran the four scriptural themes that I have identified through the "most-loved" fifty hymns as compiled by another group (see www.hymns.me.uk/50-most-loved-hymns.htm). The results were nearly identical.

24. I originally had here "American evangelical churches." But the CCLI database covers all churches in America, including the Roman Catholic Church and mainline Protestant churches.

# 7

# Lord Centered: Magnifying God

*⟨✦⟩*

THERE ARE MANY important lessons that we can learn from our study of the six scriptural songs—about the use of instruments, the expression of emotion, the implementation of literary devices and the value of poetic craftsmanship, and the providential placement of the songs and its significance for biblical studies. However, the most important lesson that we should learn is that our songs today, like these songs, should be Lord centered. And so we begin our evaluation of our worship songs with this point.

## The Horizontal Element

Before I explain and illustrate what I mean by "Lord centered," let me start with an important qualification. One of the eye-opening discoveries I've made in my study of Christian hymnody is how some of the great hymns have us singing to one another, like "Come, Christians, Join to Sing" or that famous

Christmas carol, "Good Christian Men, Rejoice," or one of my favorites, "If Thou But Suffer God to Guide Thee":

> If thou but suffer God to guide thee,
> And hope in him through all thy ways,
> He'll give thee strength, whate'er betide thee,
> And bear thee through the evil days.

At first, we might think that such a focus is out of place in a worship service. But in Scripture singing to each other is not merely condoned, but in fact commanded.[1] There is very little said about music and singing in the New Testament, and what is said often turns our attention toward each other. For example, in Ephesians 5:15–21 Paul is exhorting Christians to be careful how they walk. And so he writes, "And do not get drunk with wine, for that is debauchery, but be filled with the Spirit, addressing *one another* in psalms and hymns and spiritual songs" (verses 18–19). With the Spirit in us, we are commanded to sing to "one another." In Colossians 3:16, we find almost the same command: "Let the word of Christ dwell in you richly, teaching and admonishing *one another* in all wisdom, [by] singing psalms and hymns and spiritual songs."

## The Vertical Element

So we are to sing God's songs to one another. There is to be a horizontal dimension to our singing. But, of course, there is to be a vertical dimension as well. We are to raise our hearts

1. This, of course, fits well with Paul's overall theology of worship. From his epistles we learn that the church gathers primarily for the sake of edification and encouragement, not evangelism or even exaltation—the praise of God (e.g., 1 Cor. 11–14). This same focus is found in Hebrews 10:23–25.

and voices heavenward. Augustine defined a hymn as "a song containing praise of God." He went on to say,

> If you praise God, but without song, you do not have a hymn.
> If you praise anything, which does not pertain to the glory of
> God, even if you sing it, you do not have a hymn.[2]

While Augustine's definition is narrower than the vertical dimension just discussed, it nevertheless makes the basic point of all the Songs of Scripture: no focus on God, no hymn.[3] To walk through each song we have studied is to compile indisputable evidence for this.

The word "Lord"—*Yahweh* in Hebrew—is used sixty times in the six songs! Personal pronouns for God are used in almost every line of every song. God's people sing *to* the Lord and also *about* the Lord. The excerpts below (with italics for emphasis) highlight this important observation:

> I will sing to the Lord, for *he* has triumphed gloriously;
>     the horse and his rider *he* has thrown into the sea.
> The Lord is my strength and my song,
>     and *he* has become my salvation;
> this is my *God*, and I will praise *him*,
>     my father's *God*, and I will exalt *him*.
> The Lord is a man of war;
>     the Lord is *his* name. (Ex. 15:1–3)

> For I will proclaim the name of the Lord;
>     ascribe greatness to our *God*!

2. In Andrew Wilson-Dickson, *The Story of Christian Music* (Minneapolis: Fortress, 1992), 25.

3. I think Augustine, like Paul, used the term "hymn" to refer to a poem, usually sung in praise of a deity. See Calvin M. Johansson, *Discipling Music Ministry: Twenty-first Century Directions* (Peabody, MA: Hendrickson, 1992), 125.

The *Rock*, *his* work is perfect,
    for all *his* ways are justice.
A *God* of faithfulness and without iniquity,
    just and upright is *he*. (Deut. 32:3–4)

Hear, O kings; give ear, O princes;
    to the L*ord* I will sing;
    I will make melody to the L*ord*, the *God* of Israel.
L*ord*, when *you* went out from Seir,
    when *you* marched . . .
The mountains quaked before the L*ord*,
    even Sinai before the L*ord*, the *God* of Israel.
        (Judg. 5:3–5)

My heart exults in the L*ord*;
    my strength is exalted in the L*ord*.
My mouth derides my enemies,
    because I rejoice in *your* salvation.
There is none holy like the L*ord*;
    there is none besides *you*;
    there is no rock like our *God*. (1 Sam. 2:1–2)

The L*ord* lives, and blessed be my rock,
    and exalted be my *God*, the rock of my salvation,
the *God* who gave me vengeance
    and brought down peoples under me,
who brought me out from my enemies;
    *you* exalted me above those who rose against me;
    *you* delivered me from men of violence.
For this I will praise you, O L*ord*, among the nations,
    and sing praises to *your* name.
Great salvation *he* brings to *his* king,
    and shows steadfast love to *his* anointed,
    to David and his offspring forever. (2 Sam. 22:47–51)

Though the fig tree should not blossom . . .
yet I will rejoice in the LORD;
  I will take joy in the *God* of my salvation.
GOD, the *Lord*, is my strength;
  *he* makes my feet like the deer's;
  *he* makes me tread on my high places. (Hab. 3:17–19)

As we can see from this sampling above, songs that are "Lord centered" not only use the Lord's name,[4] but also focus on him directly, singing of his attributes and actions. (And even if he is not the subject of each sentence, he is the topic of the song.) In these songs, Yahweh is addressed and adored, and thus "enlarged" or "magnified," as Mary phrased it.[5]

## Sing to Jesus as Lord

I have intentionally labeled this section "Lord centered," rather than "God centered," both to highlight the use of the covenant name (Yahweh),[6] and to include, as the New Testament does, the worship of our Lord Jesus Christ.[7]

Poetic texts in the New Testament are often thought to be "Christ hymns" or "hymn fragments" of early Christian songs

4. For the significance of God's name in public worship, see, for example, Pss. 113:1; 115:1; 145:1.

5. See the section on "The Greatness of God" in chapter 1. Cf. Psalm 34:3, "Oh, magnify the LORD with me, and let us exalt his name together!"

6. What Allan J. Hauser cites as a similarity between the Song of Moses and the Song of Deborah is true of all six scriptural songs: their focus "on the specific name of Israel's God . . . as a way of emphasizing his all-important role in victory." "Two Songs of Victory: A Comparison of Exodus 15 and Judges 5," in *Directions in Biblical Hebrew Poetry*, ed. Elaine R. Follis (Sheffield: JSOT Press, 1987), 280.

7. Another reason, more obviously, is that I will be comparing the Songs of Scripture with Christian hymns and choruses, which sing of Christ.

(Phil. 2:5–11; Col. 1:15–20; 1 Tim. 3:16; perhaps John 1:1–5, 9–11; Rom. 10:9ff.; 1 Cor. 12:3; Eph. 5:14; 2 Tim. 2:5–6; Heb. 1:3; 1 Peter 3:18c-19, 22).[8] They focus on the person and works of Jesus, highlighting to some extent his divinity. The most obvious example of the worship of "the Word made flesh" (see John 1:14) is in the Song of the Lamb (Rev. 5:9–10).[9]

I like to think of the significance of this song to its first readers in this way: Pretend you are a typical first-century, monotheistic Jew living in one of the cities to which the book of Revelation is addressed (Rev. 1:4; cf. chs. 2–3). Each day you recite the Shema: "Hear, O Israel: The LORD our God, the LORD is one" (Deut. 6:4). The Lord is *one*. Then one day a friend of yours tells you some good news: the long-awaited Messiah has come! He invites you to a meeting of Christians, and you agree to attend. During the meeting, a man stands up and reads aloud from a book called Revelation. When he comes to what we know as chapter 4, you recognize the prophetic descriptions of the Lord; they remind you of Ezekiel and Isaiah. The Lord is enthroned in glory. He is being worshipped unceasingly: "Holy, holy, holy, is the Lord God Almighty" (v. 9). The elders are exclaiming, "Worthy are you, our Lord and God, to receive glory and honor and power" (v. 11). Now, all that sounds orthodox enough. You smile with affirmation.

8. See Paul S. Jones, *Singing and Making Music* (Phillipsburg, NJ: P&R Publishing, 2006), 104. For a list of New Testament hymns, see Daniel Liderbach, *Christ in the Early Christian Hymns* (New York: Paulist Press, 1998), 42–50.

9. Ralph P. Martin states correctly, "Christology was born in the atmosphere of worship." *Worship in the Early Church* (Grand Rapids: Eerdmans, 1974), 33. Cf. Larry W. Hurtado, *At the Origins of Christian Worship: The Context and Character of Earliest Christian Devotion* (Grand Rapids: Eerdmans, 1999), 86–92. On the possible connection between the worship service (including singing) of the early church and the book of Revelation, see Oscar Cullmann's chapter on "The Gospel according to St. John and Early Christian Worship" in his *Early Christian Worship* (London: SCM, 1953).

But the man reads on (to our chapter 5), and there you encounter a certain "Lamb," which is fine, for that is a familiar image to you—the Passover lamb, etc. But wait! The elders of the previous chapter now "[fall] down before the Lamb" (v. 8), and then they sing, "Worthy is the Lamb" (v. 12; cf. v. 9). So you say, "Wait a minute, what's going on here? Who does this Lamb think he is, or who do they think he is?" Then you listen further, and in verses 13–14 everyone and everything sing, "To him who sits on the throne [i.e., God, as in chapter 4] *and to the Lamb* be blessing and honor and glory and might forever and ever!" The implication of this passage is unmistakable. Here the Father *and the Lamb* are worshipped and glorified; therefore, the Lamb (Jesus) is viewed as divine!

After Paul performed a miracle in the city of Lystra, he and Barnabas were hailed as gods. But they weren't very keen on this idea of being worshipped. In fact, they were so upset by it all that they "tore their garments" and protested (and I paraphrase), "Have you gone mad? We're not gods any more than you are" (see Acts 14:8–17).[10] Well, here in Revelation 5, the whole world is on its knees worshipping Jesus, and there is no protest. There's no tearing of garments, and there's no objection. Why? Because Jesus is divine—the Lord! He is to be worshipped.[11] That is the scandalous particularity of Christianity.

And so when we say our songs are to be Lord centered, we have in view more than a generic God-centeredness. In a

10. See Revelation 22:8–9, where John falls down to worship at the feet of the angel who showed him these visions. And there the angel says, "You must not do that! I am a fellow servant with you. . . . Worship God."

11. It is no wonder that Christian commentators make much of this, as Greg Beale does, for example, when he highlights how these three hymns (in vv. 9–10, 12, and 13) emphasize "Jesus' deity more than most other passages in the New Testament." G. K. Beale, *The Book of Revelation*, NIGTC (Grand Rapids: Eerdmans, 1999), 358.

culture not unlike Greco-Roman and Canaanite cultures, we need definition. And in a world where people use Jesus' name as a swear word, and in a world where cults and false religions label him but a man or a teacher or a prophet, we ought to worship him through song for who he is, "very God of very God, begotten not made, being of one substance with the Father."[12] We are to sing to this "Man," to slightly revise Pliny's observation of early Christian worship, "as to God."[13]

## The Classic Hymns

Now, when I compared this first and most crucial characteristic of the Songs of Scripture with the lyrics of the CH and the CCC, I found that both, at a surface level, fared well. When we think of some of the hymns—"All Hail the Power of Jesus' Name," "Be Thou My Vision," "Come, Thou Almighty King," "Fairest Lord Jesus," "Now Thank We All Our God," "O Worship the King," "Praise to the Lord, the Almighty," "Rejoice, the Lord Is King," "The God of Abraham Praise," as well as some of the more popular hymns of the last two centuries, such as

12. There is a saying that comes from Vincent of Lerins (d. A.D. 445), which is called the Vincentian Canon. In trying to define the catholic (i.e., universal) faith, Vincent spoke of "that faith which has been believed everywhere, always, by all." Now, to be honest, there are not many of the thousand or so Christian doctrines that can be so described, but one of them that surely can is the deity of Christ. It is accepted *everywhere* (in all regions of the world), *always* (from the earliest times until the present), and *by all* (every true Christian and even every confessing Church, whether Roman Catholic, Protestant, or Eastern Orthodox). If you call yourself a Christian, then you believe, if you believe anything, that "Jesus is Lord" (Rom. 10:9; cf. 1 Cor. 12:3).

13. See Jaroslav Pelikan, *Bach among the Theologians* (Philadelphia: Fortress, 1986). Pelikan writes of "the primitive Christian practice of addressing hymns and prayers to the person of Jesus as divine, 'Christo quasi Deo' (as the earliest pagan description of the Christian community says)" (p. 7).

"Great Is Thy Faithfulness," "Crown Him with Many Crowns," and "How Great Thou Art"—we recognize that these titles alone suggest a Lord-centeredness. And, in general, God is the center of the top twenty-five CH.

Examples of this focus abound. Think of all the "alleluias" (forty in the original version) which end each line of "Christ the Lord Is Risen Today."[14] Consider also the opening stanza of "All Hail the Power of Jesus' Name":

> All hail the power of Jesus' Name!
> Let angels prostrate fall;
> Bring forth the royal diadem,
> And crown him Lord of all.

Add to these hymns the closing stanzas of "Come, Thou Almighty King" and "Praise to the Lord":

> To the great One in Three
> Eternal praises be,
> Hence evermore.
> His sovereign majesty
> May we in glory see,
> And to eternity
> Love and adore!

> Praise to the Lord! O let all that is in me adore him!
> All that hath life and breath, come now with praises before him.

So, yes, these hymns get more than a passing grade in regard to this first characteristic of the scriptural songs. They sing to and/ or about the Lord, magnifying his attributes and actions.

---

14. Remember that "alleluia" comes from a Hebrew word meaning "praise the Lord." "Yah" (at the end of "alleluia") is the shortened form of "Yahweh."

The only way a few of the hymns fail, when compared to the songs we have studied, is that the focus of the praise, while intensely personal, sometimes shifts from who God is to what God has done for us; the emphasis falling on the "for us" or "for me." I will explore this potential focusing on self in the next section of this chapter and the need to sing of God's works *in salvation history* (not just *in me*) in the next chapter.[15] For now, to get the gist of my slight critique, simply sing through a hymn like "Amazing Grace" and ask, "Who is the focus?" The answer is not simply "God and his grace."[16]

## The Contemporary Christian Choruses

Now, that minor criticism aside, the CH score quite well on this first scriptural theme. So do the CCC—or so it seems.

In *Contemporary Worship Music: A Biblical Defense*, theologian John Frame has pointed out that "the proportion of songs in [contemporary worship music] devoted primarily to praise [of God] is far greater . . . than the proportion in traditional hymnody."[17] In one sense, I agree with that

15. You might be surprised to see how much the language of self is found in the CH (and even more so in gospel songs of the last century). The lines "This is my story, this is my song," or "Jesus, lover of my soul," are good examples of how the person and work of God can sometimes be lost in the language of self. Indeed, most of the hymns in the three best-selling hymnals on amazon.com (all solid, evangelical hymnals) focus not on what God did in history, but rather on what he does in "me." Too often our peace, comfort, joy, healing, guidance, assurance, etc., do not come through any of the work of Christ, notably on the cross. Of course, it is good to sing of the personal effects of the gospel, but not at the expense of singing about the gospel itself.

16. Compare the lyrics of "O Could I Speak the Matchless Worth" with those of "Amazing Grace." Both hymns use many personal pronouns, but the emphasis in the first song clearly is God.

17. John M. Frame, *Contemporary Worship Music: A Biblical Defense* (Phillipsburg, NJ: P&R Publishing, 1997), 31–32.

assessment. If you compared all the hymns with all the choruses, you would find more choruses than hymns which sing directly to God, and possibly more which sing directly of his attributes.[18] Yet, when comparing the top twenty-five hymns with the top fifty choruses, this distinction is barely noticeable. Thus, I would remove Frame's modifying phrase, "far greater." The two groups are very similar. Both focus on God, which is good to see.

However, with the top fifty choruses sung over nearly the last decade (2000–2008), the picture is not as pretty as it first appears. You would think that with titles like "Awesome God," "Blessed Be Your Name," "Celebrate Jesus," "Everlasting God," "Glorify Thy Name," "Great Is the Lord," "He Is Exalted," "Holy Is the Lord," "How Great Is Our God," "I Exalt Thee," "Jesus, Name Above All Names," "Lord, I Lift Your Name on High," "Shout to the Lord," "You Are My King," and "You're Worthy of My Praise," there would be little room for criticism. Yet the failure of some of the contemporary songs is the failure of definition and emphasis, and thus the critique which follows is justified.

This failure of definition is most important, and I will deal with it in fuller detail in the next chapter. Here I will simply say that the lyrics of the CCC do indeed focus on God, calling us to call upon, exalt, and love him, and yet very often they fail to define who God is, as Scripture does, through his works. I would like to give the songwriters the benefit of the doubt, and say that they are working with an assumed knowledge, yet this is probably not true. The average Christian's knowledge of Scripture and basic theology today is less than it was two

---

18. To give you an example of this distinction, just think of all the hymns written on topics like the Bible, the church, and evangelism. Those songs don't directly praise God. That's perhaps the point Frame is making.

hundred years ago—and so too, judging by their lyrics, is the knowledge of today's popular lyricists.[19]

The other blemish that mars the beauty of these lyrics is that their God-centered language is often confused, if not nullified, by the language of self. We found just a touch of this, as I mentioned, in the top hymns. But here in the CCC this emphasis is more pronounced.

Here's what I mean. First we have some language issues or emphases. In the top fifty, the most repeated phrase is "my heart."[20] Now, of course, there is nothing wrong with that phrase. After all, it occurs fifty-one times in the Psalms, and twice in the six Songs of Scripture.[21] Yet, when that phrase is repeated more than phrases like "God's heart," "Jesus died," or even "my Jesus" or "my Lord," it shows, at the very least, a slightly misplaced emphasis.

We can add to this misplaced emphasis the overuse of the words "I," "me," and "my." These words dominate the titles and lyrics of these songs. Five of the fifty songs begin with the word "I."[22] To those may be added "Here I Am to Worship"

19. I say this because most of the songs lack basic theological clarity, and they too often misuse scriptural phrases or misunderstand sacred history (e.g., "Days of Elijah"). Rarely are we given any teaching on the cardinal doctrines of the Christian faith. For example, other than the Trinitarian structure of "Glorify Thy Name" and one line from "How Great Is Our God," we have no other teaching on the Trinity. So, in my opinion, cardinal doctrines, such as the Trinity, are either not understood, which shows ignorance, or they are not emphasized or taught clearly, which shows carelessness. When we cannot put together even 10 percent of the Children's Catechism from the texts of these songs, we have a major "knowledge" problem.

20. I included "my heart's," as in "my heart's desire," in the count. But I did not include "your heart," "this heart," "my spirit," or "my soul."

21. However, the phrase is not used much elsewhere in Scripture. And it should also be noted how the psalmists sometimes speak of their hearts: e.g., "My flesh and my heart may fail, but God is the strength of my heart" (Ps. 73:26), and "O LORD, my heart is not lifted up" (Ps. 131:1).

22. Seven songs begin with "I" in the top sixty.

and "Lord, I Lift Your Name on High," as well as "Change My Heart, O Lord," "Draw Me Close," "He Has Made Me Glad," "Lord, Reign in Me," "My Life Is in You," "Open the Eyes of My Heart," "Trading in My Sorrows," "You Are My All in All," "You Are My King," and "You're Worthy of My Praise."

Now, thankfully, at times these personal pronouns are used appropriately—to articulate transparency, vulnerability, dependence, and fault—like the references to self in the Psalms, the opening words of the Song of Hannah, and other biblical texts.[23] However, this is overshadowed by some seemingly self-focused lyrics, such as the notion that I am God's "desire" (in "Majesty") and that Christ, during his death, thought of "me" above everyone and everything, even and especially God's glory (in "Above All").[24] Now, I say "seemingly" only to give these Christian songwriters a charitable interpretation. I doubt that any of them wrote those lyrics to promote self above God.[25] Yet, good intentions aside, these lyrics can and do promote an unnecessary and unscriptural self-focus.

23. See, for example, the use of "my" in "Shout to the Lord" and "Lord I Lift Your Name on High." Peter Enns writes, "Many psalms are in the singular but were no doubt intended for corporate use (e.g., Ps. 89:1; 101:1; 108:1)." *Exodus*, NIVAC (Grand Rapids: Zondervan, 2000), 296. Cf. Brevard S. Childs, *The Book of Exodus: A Critical, Theological Commentary*, OTL (Louisville: Westminster, 1974), 249–50, and John D. Witvliet's section on "Individual and Communal Speech" in *The Biblical Psalms in Christian Worship: A Brief Introduction and Guide to Resources* (Grand Rapids: Eerdmans, 2007), 26–27.

24. The irony of some of the so-called God-centered praise songs is rich. See examples such as "I Could Sing of Your Love Forever," "The Heart of Worship," "Breathe," "Trading in My Sorrows," "Above All," and, to a certain extent, "He Has Made Me Glad." The song "Friend of God" starts with a quote from Psalm 8, "Who am I that you are mindful of me?" but then, so unlike the psalm, emphasizes something other than the royal dignity of man. It emphasizes that God's thoughts are on "me" because we are friends.

25. Bob Kauflin's response to his friend Paul Baloche's song "Above All" may be read in his *Worship Matters: Leading Others to Encounter the Greatness of God* (Wheaton, IL: Crossway, 2008), 224–25.

Even songs that focus on the cross (e.g., "You Are My King") are also centered on "me." "I," "my," and "me" are in nearly every line of that song. There is, of course, tremendous value to the personal application of the cross to "my" life, which a few of these songs, following in the tradition of the CH, emphasize. However, the consistent reference to self in relation to everything that God has done leads me to conclude, as I said earlier, that in singing "Jesus died for me," the CCC often focus on the "for me" rather than the "Jesus died." Again, to be clear, the problem is not the use of personal pronouns. The six Songs of Scripture, as well as the Psalms, are filled with personal pronouns.[26] Rather, the issue is focus. Who is the ultimate focus—me or God? Who is "made large"? In the scriptural songs, the focus is always clear. In the CCC, the focus is either unclear or clearly on us. This makes us "too big" and God "too small."

So, without giving "a superficial attention to the texts," as John Frame rightly claims many critics have done,[27] my study of the top choruses confirms some critics' suspicions: the CCC have an intense focus on the self. Whatever is right and true about the focus on God of these choruses is tempered by this focus on oneself.[28]

In his book *Select Hymns* (1761), John Wesley gives seven standards for "inspired singing," the seventh of which is, "Above all sing spiritually." He goes on to define that trait in this way: "Have an eye to God in every word you sing. Aim at pleasing Him more than yourself, or any other creature." This standard,

26. The six Songs of Scripture are very personal, and thus often use personal pronouns, as do many of the psalms. Yet in those scriptural songs you are never left wondering who is big and who is small. The Lord is always "large"!

27. Frame, *Contemporary Worship Music*, 32.

28. See the chapter "Humanistic Trends in Worship and Music," in Calvin M. Johansson, *Discipling Music Ministry: Twenty-first Century Directions* (Peabody, MA: Hendrickson, 1992), 45–58.

which is a perfectly biblical one, is hard to accomplish if the words we sing are more about "me" than "him"—more about "my heart" than "his holiness."

## The Song of the Golden Calf

I don't know if it is entirely kind or fair, but sometimes a few of our popular hymns and many of our popular choruses remind me of the story of the golden calf. One theological question raised in that episode is this: can we sing to Yahweh and yet be idolatrous?[29] Exodus 32:15–20 answers affirmatively:

> Then Moses turned and went down from the mountain with the two tablets of the testimony in his hand, tablets that were written on both sides; on the front and on the back they were written. The tablets were the work of God, and the writing was the writing of God, engraved on the tablets. When Joshua heard the noise of the people as they shouted, he said to Moses, "There is a noise of war in the camp." But he said, "It is not the sound of shouting for victory, or the sound of the cry of defeat, but the sound of *singing* that I hear." And as soon as he came near the camp and saw the calf and the dancing, Moses' anger burned hot, and he threw the tablets out of his hands and broke them at the foot of the mountain. He took the calf that they had made and burned it with fire and ground it to

29. In Exodus 32:2–5, after the golden calf is fashioned, Aaron builds an altar before the calf and makes this proclamation: "Tomorrow shall be a feast to *the* Lord" (v. 5). The Lord then tells Moses, "Go down, for your people, whom you brought up out of the land of Egypt, have corrupted themselves. They have turned aside quickly out of the way that I commanded them. They have made for themselves a golden calf and have worshiped it and sacrificed to it and said, 'These are your gods, O Israel, who brought you up out of the land of Egypt!'" (vv. 7–8).

powder and scattered it on the water and made the people
of Israel drink it.

The last time Moses heard "the sound of singing" and saw
the movement of dancing, it was the *Te Deum* of Triumph
(Ex. 15), a God-inspired song which exalted the Lord for his
deliverance from Egypt and its powers. In Exodus 32:15–20,
he hears a new song to Yahweh, but it is a false song. The
people are singing of their deliverance from Egypt (vv. 4, 8),
but without the law to properly define the person of God, they
are bowing down and worshipping a golden calf—the creation,
instead of the Creator.

Now, I am not asserting that our most popular worship
songs are exactly like the song that was sung to the golden calf.
But I am claiming that we are in danger of falling into the same
idolatry. We might be surprised at what or to whom most people
sing on Sunday morning, when they do so without a proper
definition of the person of God.

We are to sing to the Lord as he is revealed in Scripture. We
are to sing of his name. We are to sing of his person. We are to
sing of his works. We are to magnify him and him alone! The
Songs of Scripture provide for us the perfect model and perhaps
the perfect goad.

# 8

# The Acts of the Lord: Recalling Salvation History

THE SECOND THEME naturally follows and complements the first: our songs, like the Songs of Scripture, should exalt the *actions* of the Lord as well as his attributes.

The six songs in our study all speak of God's acts in history— of creation, the election of Israel, the exodus, the giving of the law, the establishment of David's kingdom, exilic judgment, and restoration. The Lord is either the subject of each sentence or the main protagonist of each poem: *He* cast the armies of Egypt into the Red Sea (Ex. 15). *He* found, loved, and guided Israel in the wilderness (Deut. 32). *He* triumphed over the Canaanites (Judg. 5). *He* opened up the barren womb (1 Sam. 2), and *he* lifted up his anointed (2 Sam. 22). *He* marched to war, and *he* threshed the nations in anger (Hab. 3). In all six songs—I'll say it this bluntly—God's people don't sing to God without singing about what he has done.

# New Songs on an Old Theme

Interestingly, but not surprisingly, the songs of the New Testament follow this same pattern. In these texts,[1] Christians are encouraged to sing of the person and always the works of Christ—of his incarnation, life, passion, death, resurrection, ascension, and exaltation.[2] The book of Revelation again provides the pattern, and the verses below a summary:

> Great and amazing are *your deeds*, O Lord God the Almighty!
> Just and true are *your ways*, O King of the nations! Who will

1. Again, see Phil. 2:5–11; Col. 1:15–20; 1 Tim. 3:16; and possibly John 1:1–5, 9–11; Rom. 10:9ff.; 1 Cor. 12:3; Eph. 5:14; 2 Tim. 2:5–6; Heb. 1:3; 1 Peter 3:18c–19, 22.
2. The works of Christ are reenacted by the fivefold structure of traditional eucharistic prayers. See Sofia Cavaletti, "The Jewish Roots of Christian Liturgy," in *The Jewish Roots of Christian Liturgy*, ed. Eugene J. Fisher (New York: Paulist Press, 1990), 26. Cf. the famous late fourth or early fifth century Latin hymn, "Te Deum laudamus":

> O God, we praise you,
> As Lord we confess you.
> Eternal Father, all the earth reveres you.
> The angels, the heavens and all the powers,
> The cherubim and seraphim unceasingly proclaim:
> Holy, holy, holy is the Lord God of hosts.
> Heaven and earth are full
> Of your majesty and glory.
> You are a glorious King, O Christ,
> The Father's eternal Son;
> Yet at your coming to take upon you
> The human nature that you would release,
> A virgin's womb had no dismay for you.
> Drawing death's sting,
> You opened the kingdom of heaven
> To all who would believe.
> You sit at God's right hand,
> Sharing the Father's glory;
> And we believe that you will come and judge us.

not fear, O Lord, and glorify your name? For you alone are holy. All nations will come and worship you, for *your righteous acts* have been revealed. (15:3–4)

## The Classic Hymns

Thankfully, a few of the CH do not neglect this characteristic. Some celebrate the works of God in salvation history. In fact, these songs sometimes follow the pattern found in 1 Timothy 3:16—which mentions many of the important "works" of Jesus' ministry:[3]

> Great indeed, we confess, is the mystery of godliness: He was manifested in the flesh [incarnation], vindicated by the Spirit [death], seen by angels [resurrection], proclaimed among the nations, believed on in the world [Pentecost and its aftermath], taken up in glory [ascension].[4]

For example, Christ's death, exaltation, return, and judgment are recounted in "Rejoice, the Lord Is King," and his death and resurrection in "Christ the Lord Is Risen Today." Sometimes a work of Christ (most often his death) is used by these hymn writers as a path to personal reflection—a celebration of sorts of one's own regeneration, faith, love, and service. Examples of

3. Cf. the outlines for the apostolic sermons in Acts. They often include God as Creator, Jesus as Judge and Savior through his death and resurrection, and the need for repentance and faith. Luke begins Acts by telling us that his gospel "dealt with all that Jesus began to *do* and teach" (1:1), and the first sermon he records ends with its original audience saying, "We hear them telling in our own tongues the mighty works of God" (2:11).

4. See R. Kent Hughes and Bryan Chapell, *1 and 2 Timothy and Titus*, PTW (Wheaton, IL: Crossway, 2000), 93–96. For further study of other views, see I. Howard Marshall, *Pastoral Epistles* (ICC; Edinburgh: T&T Clark, 1999), 521–29.

this would be "Jesus, Lover of My Soul" and "Amazing Grace," and the "nonclassic" but famous hymns "Jesus Paid It All" and "To God Be the Glory."[5]

Yet, sadly and surprisingly, the theme "great things he hath done," in the refrain of "To God Be the Glory," is not as common as one might expect. And the structure of "How Great Thou Art" is rare. That hymn calls us, in verse 1, to "consider all the works" of God, and then, in the remaining verses, recounts God's work in creation and salvation.

So, some of the classics sing of "the old, old story," but almost no content is given to this story. Two examples from CH should suffice. The first is "Now Thank We All Our God." This wonderful thanksgiving hymn does well when it comes to relating God's "countless gifts of love," yet they do not include Jesus' death, resurrection, or ascension (Eph. 4:7–8).[6] The other example is "Praise to the Lord, the Almighty." In the original lyrics, the first lines of the five middle verses (yes, there are seven verses) are promising because the pattern of each is, "Praise to the Lord, who . . ." The "who" is important, for with this structure we could potentially sing of the Lord *who* created the heavens and the earth, *who* holds the world together, *who* came to earth, *who* lived and healed and taught, *who* suffered, *who* died, *who* was buried, *who* rose from the grave, *who* gave the Holy Spirit, *who* ascended into heaven, *who* now sits in heavenly glory, and *who* will come again to judge the living and the dead. Yet the only acts of our Lord that are recounted are how marvelously he has made us, and how he, in specific ways, helps us in our

5. By "nonclassic" I simply mean hymns that are not in what I have classified as the top twenty-five CH.

6. Here's another example. "Holy, Holy, Holy" is one of my favorite hymns. And it gets high marks when it comes to exalting the attributes of God—holiness, power, love, etc. Yet the works of God are missing. We sing, "All thy works shall praise thy name," but we are never told what those works are.

earthly pilgrimages. All this is nice, yet it does not qualify, in my mind, as a pure connection between the person and works of Jesus as emphasized in the scriptural songs.

Too often popular hymnody recalls the general works of God in creation, but ignores his specific works of salvation history (except for his work on the cross, which gets its proper emphasis).[7] There is nothing wrong with praising God for the beauty of the earth, the heavens, flowers, human love, time, pleasures, friends, and the church (as in "For the Beauty of the Earth"), but we should not do so to the exclusion of the exodus, the incarnation, the resurrection, and Christ's return.

In the top twenty-five CH, there are only four songs that mention or allude to Christ's birth. There are no songs about his earthly ministry (his miracles, teachings, etc.).[8] And there are only two songs that mention his resurrection and return. These low numbers are very telling—and, for me, very depressing.[9]

7. By "popular hymnody" I refer to the top twenty-five, but also to hundreds of others.

8. In his thoughtful ordination paper, Todd Wilson, in footnote 24, says: "The [cross is the] wellspring, yet not the *totality* of salvation. As much as I resonate with and, in principle, affirm the sentiment of Charles Spurgeon—'My sole hope for Heaven lies in the full atonement made upon Calvary's cross for the ungodly. On that I firmly rely. I have not the shadow of a hope anywhere else' (*The Early Years*, p. 81)—the saving work of Christ cannot be reduced to the atonement, as is frequently done within Protestant Dogmatics. For the New Testament explicitly ascribes saving significance to the *entirety* of Christ's existence: his incarnation, life, death, resurrection, intercession and return. Hence, my understanding of the doctrinal loci of the 'work of Christ' includes more than the death of Christ" (p. 25). Good examples of hymns that recount well the events of Jesus' life and ministry are Rusty Edwards's "Praise the One Who Breaks the Darkness," found in *The Celebration Hymnal: Songs and Hymns for Worship* (Nashville: Word Music/Integrity Music, 1997), #293; Benjamin Russell Hanby's "Who Is He in Yonder Stall?" and John Wilbur Chapman's "One Day," found in *The Christian Life Hymnal* (Peabody, MA: Hendrickson, 2006), #145 and #150, respectively.

9. Recently, I have read through a good number of contemporary hymnals, and on the basis of that research I can add that what is characteristic of the top twenty-five CH is very much characteristic of today's hymnody. In evangelical hymnals, there are

# The Contemporary Christian Choruses

I am glad to say that there is a trend in some newer songs—notably in the work of Kristyn and Keith Getty (and with them, Stuart Townend)—which is refocusing on the works of God. Songs like "In Christ Alone," which has recently hit the top twenty-five on the CCLI charts, are a breath of fresh air.[10] This song does what Christian songs should do. With each verse, we are walked through what are arguably the four key works of Christ:

> Incarnation—"In Christ alone! who took on flesh"
> Death—"Till on that cross as Jesus died"
> Resurrection—"Up from the grave he rose again!"
> Return—"Till he returns or calls me home"

Yet, sadly, this song is the exception, rather than the rule, among the top fifty choruses.

As we have seen, we cannot simply say, "The old hymns are good; the new choruses are bad." Yet I must say that, when it comes to singing about the works of God, the adjective "bad" would be quite appropriate, except for this Getty/Townend song. To say that in the top fifty CCC the connection between God's attributes and his actions is never made would be an exaggeration, but only a slight one.

---

few songs that speak of the works of God in general, and almost none that are what I'll call "historical-narrative" songs. That is, unlike some of the psalms (e.g., Ps. 105) and biblical prayers (e.g., Neh. 9) and our six songs, they do not retell the story of an historical event or a group of events (as Stephen does, for example, in Acts 7, where he walks through much of Israel's history).

10. Another refreshing Getty/Townend song, as it relates to the person and works of Christ, is "Across the Land." From my perspective, this song—with its high and far-ranging Christology and inclusion of Jesus' miracles—is at the top of the charts with respect to this characteristic.

# Learning History through Historical Songs

Douglas Stuart, commenting on Exodus 15, talks about the generations learning "some of their history through music."[11] But Christians cannot learn much Bible history by singing the songs of the CCC. I could take my examples from nearly any of the top fifty, but I have chosen one favorite song and another promising one.

The first song is "I Love You, Lord." Due to its simplistic but singable melody, and lyrics that invoke childlike joy, trust, and adoration, this is one of my favorite contemporary choruses. We all know it. It begins like Psalm 18:2, "I love you, Lord" (NAB), and goes on to sing of lifting our voices to worship our King. I often select this as one of the songs for my congregation to sing, especially on a Communion Sunday. And I usually follow it with that wonderful, devout hymn, "My Jesus, I Love Thee." I find this juxtaposition not only pleasing to the ear—as one song thematically and musically flows into the other—but also (and to the point) a theological necessity.

What I mean is this: The song "I Love You, Lord" does a good job of praising God for who he is. But that's where it stops. Unlike the biblical text upon which it is based, Psalm 18 (cf. 2 Samuel 22—the Song of David, no less!), this chorus fails to tell us why we are to love the Lord. Psalm 18 (and the hymn "My Jesus, I Love Thee," for that matter) is completely different. As a whole, it explains, by meditating on the works of God in salvation history, why we are to love the Lord. In the psalm, David recounts the works of God in his personal and public life. He

---

11. Douglas Stuart, *Exodus*, NAC (Nashville: Broadman & Holman, 2006), 347. On the value of learning Bible history, see John Piper's small but thoughtful chapter, "The Value of Learning History: A Lesson from Jude," in *Life as a Vapor* (Sisters, OR: Multnomah, 2004), 93–96.

sings of his God, who has saved him from his enemies and has exalted him as king. "*For this* I will praise you, O LORD." That's how that psalm ends (v. 49). It begins, "I love you, O LORD" (v. 1). And then every verse that falls between the first and final verses recalls the reasons for such love. I love you, Lord—let me tell you why; let me sing of your works!

The other example is "Forever." Its refrain, "His love endures forever," is taken from Psalm 136, yet the difference between the two songs is remarkable. Psalm 136 speaks of God's specific acts (his "great wonders"), such as his creation of the heavens (sun, moon, and stars) and the earth (vv. 5–8), his Passover deliverance from Egypt (vv. 10–12) through the Red Sea (vv. 13–15), his leading (v. 16) and provision (v. 25) in the wilderness (v. 16), his victories over Israel's foes and his conquering of Canaan (vv. 17–22).[12] "Forever," quoting Deuteronomy 4:34, does mention that God has "a mighty hand and outstretched arm," and speaks of the rising and setting sun. But that is the limit of God's actions. So we are told to sing to God because "his love endures forever." Yet, as is typical of the CCC, we are only vaguely told why. We are left to wonder who this God is and why we are called to worship him.

Unfortunately, we are left with that question in most of these songs, including "The Heart of Worship." Despite that title, we are given no definition of the "Jesus" who is at the heart of our worship. We learn nothing about him in this song. I suppose that would be acceptable if the other songs sung during a church service filled in the blanks, but most of the top fifty songs, like "I Love You, Lord" and "Forever," do not.

---

12. The works, acts, or wonders of God are also recounted in Psalms 77, 78, 105, 106, 107, 111, 134, 136, and 147. The idea behind the refrain of Psalm 107 is not uncommon: "Let them thank the LORD for his steadfast love, for his wondrous works to the children of men!"

## Authentically Christian Songs?

In fact (and I say this with some reservation and humility), I question whether most of the top fifty CCC should even be considered as authentically Christian. Many of them lack basic theological definition. Of the top fifty songs, at least thirty-one are not distinctly Christian; that is, they say nothing about Jesus' birth, life, passion, death, burial, resurrection, ascension, exaltation, session, mediation, or return.[13] To make the point, some of them could be sung by some of the earliest Christian heretics. Test them for yourselves. Sing a few songs through as an Arian, Docetist, or Manichaean. You might even try them out as an Orthodox Jew or a Muslim! They would be able to sing them without objection.

Furthermore, if you replace the name "Jesus," "God," or "Lord" with the name of your boyfriend or girlfriend, or spouse, you would have a nice love song, fit for a cheesy Valentine's Day card. Try it with "Draw Me Close"—with this song, you

13. These thirty-one songs are: "As the Deer," "Better Is One Day," "Blessed Be Your Name," "Breathe," "Draw Me Close," "Everlasting God," "Forever," "Friend of God," "God of Wonders," "Great Is the Lord," "He Has Made Me Glad," "He Is Exalted," "Holy Is the Lord," "I Could Sing of Your Love Forever," "I Exalt Thee," "I Give You My Heart," "I Love You, Lord," "I Will Call upon the Lord," "Indescribable," "Lord, Reign in Me," "More Precious Than Silver," "My Life Is in You," "Open Our Eyes," "Open the Eyes of My Heart," "Shout to the Lord," "The Heart of Worship," "This Is the Day," "Trading in My Sorrows," "We Bring a Sacrifice of Praise," "We Fall Down," and "You're Worthy of My Praise." While some of these songs are acceptable theologically (e.g., "I Love You, Lord"), there is still nothing distinctly Christian about them. I give the benefit to the doubt to "Come, Now Is the Time to Worship," for a line paraphrased from Philippians 2:10–11; to "Give Thanks," for its line expressing gratitude to God for giving us his Son; to "Jesus, Name Above All Names," for its use of four biblical titles of Christ which relate to his work; and to "Shine, Jesus, Shine," for its one allusion to Christ's work on the cross. Also, to be generous, I consider songs with Trinitarian theology or reference, such as "Glorify Thy Name" and "How Great Is Our God," as distinctly Christian.

don't even need to replace names, for God is never mentioned. Or try singing the chorus of "Beautiful One" or many lines from "Breathe," "The Heart of Worship," or "Open Our Eyes," this way. The earliest Christians would have called such songs Gnostic.[14] I think they are more narcissistic than Gnostic, but both terms would be accurate.

However, three other songs may be considered acceptable as tested by Scripture. I do not commend these songs poetically or musically, but I do acknowledge that they celebrate and sing of the Lord's works.[15] "In Christ Alone" is the first of four distinctively Christian songs that sing of Christ's works. The second is "Lord, I Lift Your Name on High." This song speaks of Christ's incarnation, cross, burial, and ascension. The third is "You Are My King." The important word "because," which is left out of most songs today, is used. This word is important because it links Christ's actions with our salvation:

> I'm forgiven *because* you were forsaken
> I'm accepted, [*because*] You were condemned
> I'm alive and well
> Your spirit is within me
> *Because* you died and rose again.

The fourth and final song is "You Are My All in All," which has a refrain based on John 1:29, 36 and Revelation 5:12. We

14. These songs resemble Gnosticism because of their emphasis on the "spiritual" over against the material and/or historical. Songs like "Open the Eyes of My Heart," "The Heart of Worship," "I Could Sing of Your Love Forever," "Breathe," "Trading in My Sorrows," and "God of Wonders" could be classified as Gnostic for this reason.

15. The other fifteen songs I put in a gray category. They are Christian lyrics in that they sing (in at least one line) of Christ and/or his works, yet "gray" in that they have little value in teaching, explaining, or even applying basic Christian truths. I do not commend them, but neither do I condemn them.

sing of Jesus as "the Lamb of God," whose name is "worthy." Besides this refrain, however, there is only one other line of distinctly Christian theology in the song, a line which focuses on how Christ's cross atones for sin and shame.[16]

Now, it gets a little scary if that is the fourth most "Christian" praise song sung in today's churches! It is even scarier to consider that I could write on less than half a sheet of paper each and every distinctly Christian reference in those songs. And it gets really, really scary if I can count on my fingers and toes (with eight toes left over) the number of songs in the top fifty which refer to the essential acts of our Lord Jesus' earthly ministry. Here's how many times the following acts of Jesus Christ are sung about in forty-six of fifty of the top CCC:[17]

Incarnation—three times (all very vaguely)
Life—once (again, vaguely)
Death—four times
Resurrection—twice
Return—twice

## Musical Matters Matter

If you have a robe, now is the time to rend it! Any ashes? Throw them on your head. For this is as serious an error as any in the church over the last two centuries, one in which sorrow and repentance should be our only response. And yet, what do

16. Two good choruses on the works of Christ which are not found in the top fifty are "He Is Lord," by Linda Lee Johnson et al. and "At the Name of Jesus," by Caroline M. Noel. These songs can be found in *The Hymnal for Worship and Celebration* (Nashville: Word, 1986), #105 and #235.

17. If an act (e.g., Jesus' death) is mentioned more than once in a song, that song is counted only once.

most of us do? We sit on the sidelines, saying glibly of these songs, "That's a cool chorus," or "What a catchy tune!" or "Aw, come on, what does music matter?" Well, such musical matters do matter to God! And we know this because of what he has taught and demonstrated in his Word. The God-breathed Songs of Scripture do not (like some of the CH and most of the CCC) praise God in the abstract or even solely praise his divine attributes. Instead, they always connect the Actor with his actions, his character with his works.

If you like bumper sticker theology, here are two slogans to remember what the scriptural songs teach on this second theme:

No Know Works; No Know God
Know Works; Know God

Without the works of God, we do not know him. So, as nice as it is to sing, "Oh give thanks to the LORD" (Psalm 105:1a), we must add, "make know his deeds among the peoples!" (v. 1b). And, as wonderful as it is to bellow out with hands raised and hearts engaged, "Sing to him, sing praises to him" (v. 2a), we must always add, "tell of all his wondrous works!" (v. 2b). Our great God is worshipped and adored when, and only when, we sing of his mighty acts in salvation.

# 9

# Joy over Justice: Rejoicing in God's Just Judgments

⟨∾⟩

IN MUSIC, there is something called a melodic line. A melody is a particular, identifiable association of notes and pitches—what we often call a "tune." A *melodic line* is a succession of notes forming a distinctive sequence—a tune within the tune—which brings unity to the musical piece by its reoccurrence.

Do you know what theme reoccurs throughout the Songs of Scripture? Joy in God's just judgment. That's the melodic line! Just look and listen for it in the lines from the songs below:

> I will sing to the LORD, for he has triumphed gloriously;
>   the horse and his rider he has thrown into the sea. . . .
> Sing to the LORD, for he has triumphed gloriously;
>   the horse and his rider he has thrown into the sea.
>   (Ex. 15:1, 21)

145

Rejoice with him, O heavens;
   bow down to him, all gods,
for he avenges the blood of his children
   and takes vengeance on his adversaries. (Deut. 32:43)


I will make melody to the LORD, the God of Israel [because
   God marched against the mighty Canaanites]. (Judg.
   5:3; cf. v. 13)


My heart exults in the LORD. . . .
My mouth derides my enemies. (1 Sam. 2:1)


The LORD lives, and blessed be my rock,
   and exalted be my God, the rock of my salvation,
the God who gave me vengeance
   and brought down peoples under me. (2 Sam.
      22:47–48)


Yet I will rejoice in the LORD;
   I will take joy in the God of my salvation [because God is
      saving the prophet from the wrath which will come
      upon Judah and then Babylon]. (Hab. 3:18)


Moses and Miriam, Deborah and David, Hannah and Habakkuk
all rejoiced in God's justice—when the Lord rescued or delivered
or saved them from their enemies.

   Now, if this theme was apparent only in these songs, we might
write them off as "occasional songs," that is, songs written for a
specific people and time in history, and thus not repeatable. Yet
the evidence of the rest of the songs in Scripture suggests otherwise. This melodic line is heard in other Old Testament songs,[1]

---

1. See especially the songs/poems of Isaiah 14:9; 24:7–26:21; 30:27–33; 35:1–4;
42:10, 13; 51:9–11. Cf. 1 Chron. 16:14, 33–35; 2 Chron. 20:14–27. For an overview,

including thirty-three of the Psalms.[2] Furthermore, it is also heard in every possible New Testament "song"—the Lucan canticles (Mary's Magnificat, the Benedictus of Zechariah, the angels' Gloria in Altissimis Deo, and the Nunc Dimittis of Simeon), the Christ hymns (notably Phil. 2:9–11; Col. 1:15–20; Eph. 5:14; 1 Tim. 3:16), and the songs in Revelation (5:9–10; 14:2–3; 15:3–4).[3]

With such strength and scope of evidence, it seems fair and logical to suggest that what was set to song for David's choirs (cf. the superscript of Psalm 18)[4] should also be set to song for ours. Our choirs and congregations should join in the communion of the saints by rejoicing over God's judgments, our full deliverance from all evil forces and foes.

Yet such joy, as we all know, finds little part in today's Christian corporate worship. And this is not because wrath has been removed from our official theology. You will be hard pressed to find any theologically conservative church which

---

see "Songs of Isaiah," in Herbert Lockyer Jr., *All the Music of the Bible: An Exploration of Musical Expression in Scripture and Church Hymnody* (Peabody, MA: Hendrickson, 2004), 91–106.

2. Psalms 5:10–11; 7; 9; 20:5; 21:8–13; 35:8–9, 27–28; 44:4–8; 45:3–6; 47:1–3; 54:4–7; 56:9–10; 58:10–11; 59:16 (cf. v. 13); 66:1–7; 67:4; 68:1–4, 20–26; 75; 76:10; 79:11–13; 89:1–10; 92:1–9; 96:13; 97:3, 8; 98:9; 104:34; 106:10–12; 108; 132:16–18; 135:1, 8–11, 21; 136; 145:20–21; 146:9–10; 147:1–6; 149. And remember that Christians are twice admonished in the New Testament to sing psalms (Eph. 5:19; Col. 3:16). It is highly unlikely that all of the passages in the psalms listed above should be avoided. On the use of the imprecatory psalms in the New Testament, see James E. Adams, *War Psalms of the Prince of Peace: Lessons from the Imprecatory Psalms* (Phillipsburg, NJ: Presbyterian and Reformed, 1991), 2–3.

3. Note again in Revelation 15:3 the use of the Song of Moses under the new covenant. For further discussion on this point, see the section "The Song of Moses and the Triumph of the Lamb" in chapter 1.

4. "To the Choirmaster: A Psalm of David, the Servant of the LORD, who addressed the words of this song to the LORD on the day when the LORD rescued him from the hand of all his enemies, and from the hand of Saul."

disagrees with the declaration in Hebrews 6:1–2 that "eternal judgment" is a cardinal doctrine of the Christian faith.[5] And yet, in practice, what H. Richard Niebuhr said of the social gospel early last century is (as we shall see) an apt critique of the most popular evangelical lyrics at the turn of this century: our songs sing of "a God without wrath [who] brought men without sin into a kingdom without judgment through the ministrations of a Christ without a cross."[6]

## The Classic Hymns

In the top twenty-five CH, as they are now (but not originally) printed, the theme of *joy in judgment* is absent. Even the theme of *judgment*, which in the scriptural songs is as big as a camel on your front lawn, has been swallowed up! Below I have listed *the only two* references in these hymns.

> His chariots of wrath the deep thunderclouds form.
> ("O Worship the King")

> Be of sin the double cure;
> Save from wrath and make me pure. ("Rock of Ages")

Now, if we included the original verses of the CH, we would add the following lines:

5. "Therefore let us leave the elementary doctrine of Christ and go on to maturity, not laying again a foundation of repentance from dead works and of faith toward God, and of instruction about washings, the laying on of hands, the resurrection of the dead, and *eternal judgment*" (Heb. 6:1–2).

6. H. Richard Niebuhr, *The Kingdom of God in America* (Chicago: Willett, Clark, 1937), 193.

While the firm mark of wrath divine,
His soul in anguish stood. (verse 2 of "Alas! And Did My
    Saviour Bleed")

That quenched the wrath of hostile heaven. (verse 5 of
    "And Can It Be")

With power he vindicates the just,
And treads th' oppressor in the dust. (verse 11 of "Jesus
    Shall Reign")

Jesus, our Lord, arise,
Scatter our enemies, and make them fall. (verse 2 of "Come,
    Thou Almighty King")

He sits at God's right hand till all his foes submit,
And bow to his command, and fall beneath his feet:
Lift up your heart, lift up your voice;
Rejoice, again I say, rejoice!

He all his foes shall quell, shall all our sins destroy,
And every bosom swell with pure seraphic joy;
Lift up your heart, lift up your voice;
Rejoice, again I say, rejoice! (verses 4 and 5 of "Rejoice, the
    Lord Is King!")[7]

These now rejected verses, especially the ones from the last three hymns, are perfect examples of what we should be singing. But again, why don't we?

7. Verse 4 of "Rejoice, the Lord Is King!" is printed in a few hymnals, including *The Christian Life Hymnal* (Peabody, MA: Hendrickson, 2006), 206; *Cantus Christi* (Moscow, ID: Canon Press, 2002), 326; *Trinity Hymnal* (Philadelphia: Great Commission Publications, 1961), 226.

It is not as though there are no English hymns which address this theme. Actually, there are plenty—though there could be more.[8] But our generation has chosen, intentionally or unintentionally, not to select such hymns for hymnals or congregational singing—or, if they are selected, to modify or remove the offending lyrics.[9] It is not uncommon to find in today's best-selling hymnals the word or abbreviation for "altered" inconspicuously hiding at the bottom of the page.[10] And too often the altering involves a removal of theological terms or themes, including "wrath" or "judgment."

8. The selection from English hymnody is not as large as I'd like. For example, on the Web site www.nethymnal.org, which rightly boasts of being "the #1 Hymn site since 1996," for it includes in its extensive database over ten thousand hymns, there are listed only twenty-five songs on the topic of judgment. And some of those songs are "fire and brimstone" or "turn or burn" gospel songs, which give a slightly different twist to the theme of judgment.

In one of today's most popular hymnals, *The Celebration Hymnal*, only 17 of the 750 hymns mention anything on the theme of judgment (broadly construed to include any song which mentions even one word like "foes," "angry," "judgment," "the wicked"). Most of these 17 references are one-liners; in other words, the songs are not about God's just judgments. Predictably, the Songs of Scripture are ignored, the psalm texts are neutered, battle/war themes are spiritualized, and the melodic line is absent. There are not even any judgment hymns in the section on "The Second Coming of Christ"!

What can be said of *The Celebration Hymnal* is true of the most popular hymnals of the last three decades, including *The Hymnal for Worship and Celebration* and *The Christian Life Hymnal*. However, there are some notable exemptions, such as *Trinity Hymnal* of the Orthodox Presbyterian Church and the Presbyterian Church in America. A word search on the OPC online database is revealing (see www.opc.org/search.html): of the 730 hymns, there are 5 with the word "vengeance," 24 with "wrath," 66 with "foes," 21 with "the wicked," 32 with "judgment," and 23 with "judge." I surmise that these "high" numbers are due to traditional Presbyterian inclusion of psalm texts and other lyrics reflective of the theology of the Psalms.

9. It is beyond the scope of this work to explain why or how this happened. For a thoughtful overview and critique of the loss of evangelical theology, see David Wells, *No Place for Truth, or Whatever Happened to Evangelical Theology?* (Grand Rapids: Eerdmans, 1993); Wells, *God in the Wasteland: The Reality of Truth in a World of Fading Dreams* (Grand Rapids: Eerdmans, 1994).

10. I am well aware that most editors of hymnals adapt and rearrange original texts. So I am not surprised by that, nor do I think there is no place for careful

# Removing the Wrath

To further illustrate and press this point, allow me to compare how the theme of God's wrath is used or not used by two of the church's greatest hymn writers, Isaac Watts (1674–1748) and Timothy Dudley-Smith (1926–). Of the 365 hymns in *The Psalms and Hymns of Isaac Watts*, there are over 50 that touch on the theme of judgment,[11] and a few of those include our melodic line (joy in judgment).[12] But of the 285 hymns in Dudley-Smith's *A House of Praise: Collected Hymns 1961–2001*, there are only 9 songs on judgment[13] and only a few examples of our melodic line. Of those songs on judgment, almost all of the references are one-liners.[14] And in his most recent work, *A Door for the Word: 36 New Hymns Written Between 2002 and 2005*, only three songs touch on this theme, including the first song, "A Righteous God in Heaven Reigns."[15]

---

editing. My surprise comes with reviewing what verses and words are tossed in the editor's wastebasket.

11. Watts, *The Psalms and Hymns of Isaac Watts* (Morgan, PA: Soli Deo Gloria, 1997). See Book I: Hymns 8, 13, 28, 29, 30, 38, 42, 45, 56, 58, 59, 65, 86, 87, 89, 90, 91, 98, 100, 118, 147, 148; Book II: Hymns 6, 22, 27, 44, 52, 53, 62, 80, 83, 84, 98, 103, 104, 105, 107, 111, 112, 113, 114, 115, 118, 120, 125, 155, 166, 167, 169, 170; Book III: Hymns 1, 10, 22, 85. Most of these songs do not contain merely a brief mention of judgment. Much of each of these songs deals with this theme. Hughes Oliphant Old's assessment is correct: "The work of Isaac Watts exemplifies the Reformed doxological tradition at its best. We find in his work a balance between psalmody and hymnody. The hymnody spring from the psalmody; it is inspired by the psalmody." *Worship: Reformed According to Scripture*, rev. ed. (Louisville: Westminster John Knox, 2002), 48.

12. One example of the melodic line is found in Book I: Hymn 42, which ends with the praise to God, "Thy just revenge adore." See Watts, *Psalms and Hymns*, 325.

13. See Hymns 43, 146, 153, 160, 170, 179, 185, 209, and 216 in *A House of Praise: Collected Hymns 1961–2001* (Carol Stream, IL: Hope, 2003).

14. For example, see stanza 2, line 1, of "Through Centuries Long the Prophets of Old," and stanza 2 of "The Everlasting Lord Is King."

15. This song, based on Nahum 1 (it would be hard to miss the theme of wrath in that chapter!), is by far the best of the Dudley-Smith "judgment" hymns. Verse 3 is as follows:

To find so little work on this theme is surprising—not only because Dudley-Smith is a theologically astute lyricist, but also because many of his hymns are directly based on texts of Scripture, especially the Prophets and Psalms. And what is most surprising is how his paraphrases and summaries of forty-three of the psalms (in his section on "Metrical Psalms") so often follow today's trend of removing the theme of wrath.[16] For example, in "To Heathen Dreams of Human Pride," which is an otherwise excellent song, he takes out what I call the "moral punch" of Psalm 2, its final verse:

> Kiss the Son,
>> lest he be angry, and you perish in the way,
>> for his wrath is quickly kindled.
> Blessed are all who take refuge in him. (v. 12)

While Dudley-Smith understands this psalm well, he waters down the original application with his rendering of that verse:

> His righteous indignations burn;
> as fire and flame his wrath is poured:
> in judgment swift the guilty learn
> the day of vengeance of the Lord.

Yet, in his notes on this hymn, Dudley-Smith shows his theological and method-ological hand: "I have tried," he writes, "to be true to the thrust of the book, and its vision of a righteous (and offended) God, while offering a hymn suitable for Christian worship. The occasions when it would be the right choice of hymn are probably few." *A Door for the Word* (Oxford: Oxford University Press, 2006), 41.

For a corrective to the notion that certain scriptural themes might not be suitable for regular Christian worship, see Robert L. Dabney's essay, "The Chris-tian's Duty towards His Enemies," in appendix 1 of Adams, *War Psalms of the Prince of Peace.*

16. The work of Christopher M. Idle on the Psalms is exceptional. While the theme of judgment is not often found in his other Scripture-based hymns (30 of 307 such hymns mention the theme), it pervades his psalm-based lyrics. For the best example of a contemporary lyricist dealing with the theme of joy in judgment, see *Light upon the River* (Carol Stream, IL: Hope, 1998), 217–84, and *Walking by the River* (Carol Stream, IL: Hope, 2008), 29–37.

Let humble hearts this lesson learn
and bow before his throne;
in true and trembling homage turn,
and name him Lord alone.
    O happy hearts, with wisdom blest,
    who trust in him, and in him rest![17]

He likewise removes the theme of wrath in his hymns based on
Psalm 8, where verse 2b is removed, and Psalm 95, where verse
11 is tamed.[18]

In general, I admire Dudley-Smith's work very much. But
we see how easy it is for even the most thoughtful and textual
lyricists today to have this blind spot.

## The Contemporary Christian Choruses

Now, in turning from the lines of Dudley-Smith to the lyrics
of the CCC, we turn not from apples to oranges, but from solid
coconuts, with a hole or two, to rotten squash, with, well, rot
everywhere. The way these top choruses radically neuter any and
all scriptural negatives—wrath, judgment, etc.—is sickening.

17. Compare what Watts does with the end of Psalm 2 in his three versions of
the psalm. See *Psalms and Hymns*, 3–6. One version ends,

With humble love address the Son,
Lest he grow angry, and ye die;
His wrath will burn to worlds unknown,
If ye provoke his jealousy.
His storms shall drive you quick to hell;
He is a God, and ye but dust:
Happy the souls that know him well,
And make his grace their only trust.

18. This is also done in some of the great Christian poems, such as William
Hammond's lyrics on the Song of Moses and the Lamb, "Awake, and Sing the Song."
See Philip Graham Ryken, *Exodus*, PTW (Wheaton, IL: Crossway, 2005), 401, 412.

I mentioned in chapter 5 how the CCLI database—which contains over 200,000 songs, including all of the CH and every published contemporary worship song—has only 425 songs that contain the word "wrath," and 570 the word "judgment." That compares to 36,171 songs with the word "love," 37,171 with the word "me," and 2,246 with the word "happy."[19] Back in chapter 5, I indicated how these *unlovely* stats made *me* very *unhappy*. Well, now I am more than unhappy to share with you, after examining each and every line of the top fifty songs, that they contain only three instances of the "negative" themes.

The first and best—in the sense that it is precisely the melodic line of the scriptural songs—comes from "I Will Call upon the Lord," a pithy chorus which derives its lines directly from the Song of David:

I will call upon the Lord
Who is worthy to be praised
[And I am] saved from my enemies. [2 Sam. 22:4]


The Lord liveth and blessed be [my] Rock [v. 47a, kjv]
And may [the] God . . . of my salvation be exalted.
        [v. 47b, nlt]

19. I checked www.ccli.com/LicenseHolder/Search/SongSearch.aspx on March 24, 2009. When I did a fresh word search on "love" and "me," my two computers were unable, in the allotted time, to gather the information (the point being that there were too many entries). So I asked my administrative assistant to give it a try with her new computer. It didn't work for her either. She next called her husband, but even his high-tech computer at work couldn't gather the information we desired. So she called CCLI, and they gave us the numbers. However, having done this same word study in 2007, I doubt that they gave us accurate stats, for then, with only 150,000 songs in the database, I found 40,878 songs with the word "love" and 42,144 with "me." As of January 2010, the database only allows 1000 songs to be listed at a time. For example, if you typed in "love" it would say: The following 1000 Songs were found matching "love."

The second example comes from Rich Mullins' "Awesome God," where he speaks of God's judgment on Adam and Eve and the people of Sodom.[20] The final song is (again!) "In Christ Alone." This song, which unashamedly talks of sin and the curse, adds the line, "Till on that cross as Jesus died; the wrath of God was satisfied." Even though these songs don't hit the exact notes of the melodic line, we will, at this point, take what we can get.

## A Different Gospel?

Now why is it that the Songs of Scripture sing freely about God's righteous judgment and our joy in it, while only a few lines in our top fifty choruses even mention judgment? This is not merely a deficiency; this is a grave mistake, which distorts the gospel message. Imagine the book of Romans without Paul's teaching on sin and wrath! Or think of the book of Revelation without the singing of our salvation. Do we have the gospel if we just sing about grace, freedom, peace, joy, and so on, without singing of being saved from wrath, sin, our enemies, etc.? I think not. How are we to sing "spiritual songs" (Eph. 5:19) when the words of our songs are so far removed from the work of the Spirit, which is, according to our Lord Jesus, to "convict the world concerning sin and righteousness and *judgment*" (John 16:8; cf. v. 11)?

Now, I realize that many Christians today in North America have a hard time understanding the depths of their sin and cannot comprehend what it is like to have enemies who are more than spiritual. I also know that our culture trains us to think that

---

20. It should be noted, however, that most churches sing only the chorus of this song (sometimes because that is all that is printed in the hymnal), which does not contain the lines on judgment.

155

joy and justice are not interrelated themes. And I recognize that there are tough theological tensions here: are we to sing happily of the judgment of others when Christ commanded us to love our enemies?[21] Yet when all of the Old Testament songs in our study, plus some of the psalms, the lyrics in Isaiah, and the New Testament songs all sing of this theme,[22] who are we to remove or neglect it? Shame on us!

The story of David and Goliath ends with David cutting off the head of that giant enemy of God and Israel (1 Sam. 17:50–51). The story of Esther ends with the hanging of Haman and the destruction of the enemies of God (Esth. 8:11, 17; 9:5, 16–22). And both of these narratives end with joy over judgment! We may not read about such things in children's Bibles anymore, or hear about them in sermons, or sing about them in songs, but we should.

## Irony of Ironies! All Is Irony!

As I was completing this chapter, my wife and I attended a concert of Felix Mendelssohn's *Elijah*. It was performed by two secular singing groups at a secular college's concert hall. We sat in the last row for this wonderful performance, and we listened to lyrics rise up to our ears that you will rarely (dare I say never) hear in churches today. Here's a sampling:

> Help, Lord! Help, Lord! Help, Lord!
> Wilt thou quite destroy us?

21. For further discussion of this, see chapter 1.
22. We can add the following as textual proofs: Rev. 5:9 ("seals" in chapters 6–8); 7:10; 11:15–18; 12:7–12; 15:1–16:1ff.; 18:20; 19:1–6, 11–21; also Rom. 12:19–20; 2 Thess. 1:6–10; 3:1–2; Heb. 10:13; James 5:4–5; 1 Peter 4:12–19.

Yet doth the Lord see it not,
He mocketh at us! His curse
Hath fallen down upon us.
His wrath will pursue us till
He destroy us. For he, the Lord
our God, he is a jealous God.

Is not his word like a fire?
And like a hammer that breaketh
the rock into pieces?
For God is angry with the wicked
every day. And if the wicked turn not,
the Lord will whet his sword; and he
hath bent his bow, and made it ready.[23]

"Ah, the irony," I thought to myself, as a baritone Elijah sang to me of God's wrath and as I looked over the hundreds of souls sitting and listening to the Word of God sung. How is it that believers are afraid to sing what unbelievers now sometimes sing for mere entertainment? How is it that the melodic line of the scriptural songs does not sing in our hearts today? Have we forgotten the gospel? Have we forgotten the good news, in the words of *Elijah*?

O Lord, thou hast overthrown
Thine enemies and destroyed them.

---

23. George Frideric Handel's oratorio *Deborah* (1733), with lyrics by Samuel Humphreys, is an even better example of a classical score which doesn't shy away from the theme of judgment (see especially Act 1, Scene 1:2, 10, 11; Act 2, Scene 1:25; Scene 2:32, 36, 37, 38, 42; Act 3, Scene 1:50, 57, 58, 64). In a sense, it is a whole drama about our melodic line—joy in judgment (see especially Act 3, Scene 1:52; Scene 3:65).

# 10

# Practical Wisdom: Exhorting
# Us to Godliness

A CHARACTER in Michael Cunningham's Pulitzer Prize winning novel, *The Hours*, uses two analogies for "the realm of the duped and the simpleminded." One is "Christians with acoustic guitars."[1] Now, while the book in your hands is not about acoustic guitars or electric organs—it is not about appropriate instrumentation in corporate worship[2]—it is about calling Christians out of the realm of the duped and simpleminded when it comes to the lyrical content of our songs. The point is

1. Michael Cunningham, *The Hours* (New York: Farrar, Straus and Giroux, 1998), 12.
2. Resources dealing with the issue of instrumentation in the Bible include Andrew E. Hill, *Enter His Courts with Praise! Old Testament Worship for the New Testament Church* (Grand Rapids: Baker, 1993), 290. I like what Harold M. Best points out: "The human voice is the only musical instrument that God has directly created." See his section on "The Uniqueness of the Human Voice" in *Unceasing Worship: Biblical Perspectives on Worship and the Arts* (Downers Grove, IL: InterVarsity, 2003), 143–44.

APPLICATIONS FOR CHRISTIAN WORSHIP

not that we want the world to esteem our music. Whether or
not the world asks us to "sing us one of those Christian songs,"
as Judah's captors asked them to do (see Ps. 137:3), matters little
in our present time of exile. What does matter is how well our
words reflect God's Word. So I do care about this question, the
one we have been asking in these last four chapters: what can
we do to return more to the Word in our worship?

Well, one of the ways, and the final of the four themes
I am highlighting, is to return to singing what Isaac Watts
called "moral songs," which I call "practical wisdom."[3] So,
should we sing of the Lord? Of course! And should we sing
especially of his works in salvation history? Most certainly!
And should we sing with joy over his past, present, and future
judgments? Indeed. But finally, should we sing of morals
or ethics—of avoiding this sin and doing that good work?
Again our answer is yes.

## Isn't This Moralizing?

When I was trained to preach, I was taught to avoid
moralizing a biblical text. An example of moralizing would
be to interpret the narrative about Jacob and Esau as a lesson on "the negative results of parental favoritism," rather
than on "how Abraham's family line was carried on through
Jacob and Esau."[4] Another example would be to remove the
redemptive-historical significance of the story of David and
Goliath, turning their battle into a moral allegory—making

3. See Isaac Watts, *Divine and Moral Songs for the Use of Children* (repr., Whitefish, MT: Kessinger, 2003).
4. Gordon D. Fee and Douglas Stuart, *How to Read the Bible for All Its Worth*,
3rd ed. (Grand Rapids: Zondervan, 2003), 92.

Goliath into the sins Christians must conquer by the sling of
faith and the five stones of obedience, service, Bible reading,
prayer, and fellowship.[5]

In advocating "practical wisdom," I do not mean "moralizing" Old Testament texts. Rather, I have in view applying
the morals found in these songs to our songs. I'm trying to
say what John Calvin said in his *Commentaries on the Four
Last Books of Moses*: "God never speaks except to render men
fruitful in good works."[6] Or, what Peter Craigie writes of the
Song of Yahweh (Deut. 32) summarizes well my effort. He
speaks of that song being "similar to the wisdom literature
in that it includes very practical advice (cf. vv. 7, 28–29);
its function is to remind and to educate the people in the
way they should take (cf. 31:19)—it is not simply a song
of praise."[7]

The Songs of Scripture are not simply songs of praise.
They are songs that call us to live righteously—to *put off*
pride, idolatry, immorality, and ungodly fear, and to *put on*
courage and mercy—and even to rejoice in our God-graced
righteousness ("I have kept the ways of the LORD," 2 Sam.
22:22). And in this way, they function, as Paul noted in
Colossians 3:16 they should, as "wisdom" with which we are
to teach and admonish one another.[8]

5. See Graeme Goldsworthy, *Gospel and Kingdom: A Christian Interpretation of
the Old Testament*, BCL (Carlisle, UK: Paternoster, 1994), 9–11.

6. Calvin, *Commentaries on the Four Last Books of Moses, Arranged in the Form
of a Harmony*, trans. Charles William Bingham (repr., Grand Rapids: Baker, 1979),
337. Martin Luther's "First Preface" to his hymns also points to this. He writes of
singing the spiritual songs and psalms "that thereby the word of God and Christian
doctrine be in every way furthered and *practiced*." *The Hymns of Martin Luther* (New
York: C. Scribner's, 1883), 23 (emphasis added).

7. Peter C. Craigie, *The Book of Deuteronomy*, NICOT (Grand Rapids: Eerdmans, 1976), 374.

8. Cf. 1 Cor. 10:1–14.

## The Deadliest of Sins

In the six scriptural songs, pride is the sin most often addressed.[9] In Exodus 15:9, we are told of Egypt's overconfidence:

> The enemy said, "I will pursue, I will overtake,
> I will divide the spoil, my desire shall have its fill of
> them.
> I will draw my sword; my hand shall destroy them
> [Israel]."

Note the personal pronouns—"I" (four times) and "my" (two times). Then note the change in pronouns. Speaking of God, verse 10 begins, "You." This God-centeredness, in contrast to Egypt's self-centeredness, continues through the rest of the song, as God is addressed: "You blew . . . who is like you . . . you stretched . . . you have lead . . . you have guided . . . the greatness of your arm . . . you have purchased . . . you will bring them . . . [you will] plant them . . . your abode . . . your hands have established" (vv. 10–18).

The first few lines of Thomas Moore's "Sound the Loud Timbrel," a poem based on Exodus 15, summarizes this point well:

> Sound the loud timbrel o'er Egypt's dark sea!
> Jehovah has triumphed—his people are free.
> Sing—for *the pride of the tyrant* is broken,
> His chariots, his horsemen, all splendid and brave—
> *How vain was their boast*, for the Lord hath but spoken,
> And chariots and horsemen are sunk in the wave.

9. It is also often addressed in the Psalms (see esp. 5:5; 10:2, 4; 12:3; 31:18, 23; 36:11; 40:4; 49:6; 52:1; 59:12; 73:3, 6; 75:4–5; 94:2, 4; 101:5; 123:4; 138:6; 140:5).

Pride is also addressed in the Song of Hannah. Hannah sings directly of her enemies, but indirectly to all who struggle with this sin: "Talk no more so very proudly, let not arrogance come from your mouth" (1 Sam. 2:3). Then she (like Mary, see Luke 1:48, 51–53) sings of the reversal of fortunes. If you are proud, rich, and exalted, watch out! David also sings of this theme in 2 Samuel 22:28, "You save a humble people, but your eyes are on the haughty to bring them down." And no less important, in fact—perhaps most important—the apostle Paul, in his hymn to Christ in Philippians 2:6–11, summarizes and puts an exclamation point on the necessity of humility. He sets up that song, saying in verses 3–5:

> Do nothing from rivalry or conceit, but in humility count others more significant than yourselves. Let each of you look not only to his own interests, but also to the interests of others. Have this mind among yourselves, which is yours in Christ Jesus.

## Other Deadly Sins

Besides the sin of pride, the sin of idolatry and the immoralities usually associated with it are also addressed (e.g., Deut. 32:17; Judg. 5:8). And then, beyond pride and idolatry, other vices mentioned in these six songs include forgetfulness, sloth, and gluttony (or a combination of them). In the Song of Deborah, we read of four Israelite tribes—Reuben, Gad (called "Gilead"), Dan, and Asher—and a non-Israelite people, Meroz (who were just helped by Israel), who all should have helped in battle. Instead, "they did not come to the help of the LORD" (Judg. 5:15–23). Similarly, in Deuteronomy 32:15 we read of the reasons for Israel's idolatry: "But Jeshurun grew fat and kicked; you grew fat, stout, and sleek; then he forsook God who made him and scoffed at the Rock of his salvation."

So, as made clear above, the Songs of Scripture are not simply songs of praise. They are songs that call us to live wisely.[10]

## The Classic Hymns

Thankfully, there is within Protestant hymnody a rich tradition of songs that follow this pattern. During the Reformation, it was common to write songs about the Ten Commandments, as Martin Luther, for example, did. Luther's hymn, "That Man a Godly Life Might Live," which is based on a thirteenth-century hymn used when Christians went on pilgrimages, gives a feel for this kind of moral song.[11] The first verse of thirteen is as follows:

> That man a godly life might live,
> God did these Ten Commandments give
> By His true servant Moses, high
> Upon the Mount Sinai.
> Have mercy, Lord!

Verse 9 sings of not stealing:

> Steal not; oppressive acts abhor;
> Nor wring their lifeblood from the poor;

10. I use the term "wisely" or "wise" in the way it is used in the Wisdom Literature, notably Proverbs, where true wisdom has ethical implications. The "wise" person in Proverbs is the one who fears the Lord and walks in his ways.

11. See Luther, *The Hymns of Martin Luther*, 82–86. This hymn can be found in *Cantus Christi* (Moscow, ID: Canon Press, 2002), 387–89. Luther regarded music as a teacher or pedagogue, but also as a "guardian of morals." See Carl F. Schalk, *Luther on Music: Paradigms of Praise* (St. Louis: Concordia, 1988), 32.

But open wide thy loving hand
To all the poor in the land.
Have mercy, Lord!

Typical of Luther's exegesis of the Ten Commandments,[12] each commandment is bathed in grace—"Have mercy, Lord!"—and each negative command is given a positive replacement: for example, give instead of stealing.

This type of moral singing is also found, as mentioned earlier, in Isaac Watts, the father of English hymnody. In *Divine and Moral Songs for the Use of Children*, we have songs about Christian morality. Many of the song titles summarize the themes: "Against Lying," "Against Quarrelling and Fighting," "Against Scoffing and Calling Names," "Against Cursing, Swearing, and Taking God's Name in Vain," "Against Idleness and Mischief," "Against Evil Company," "Against Pride in Clothes." Watts also includes songs on "The Ten Commandments" and "Our Saviour's Golden Rule," which are printed below:

1. Thou shalt have no more Gods but me.
2. Before no idol bow thy knee.
3. Take not the Name of God in vain:
4. Nor dare the Sabbath-day profane.
5. Give both thy parents honour due.
6. Take heed that thou no murder do.
7. Abstain from words and deeds unclean:
8. Nor steal, though thou art poor and mean:
9. Nor make a wilful lie, nor love it.
10. What is thy neighbour's dare not covet.

12. See Luther's Small and Large Catechisms.

Be you to others kind and true,
As you'd have others be to you;
And neither do nor say to men
Whate'er you would not take again.

Now, in the top twenty-five CH I found a balance very similar to the six scriptural songs.[13] As the lines of the scriptural songs speak of "practical wisdom" a small percentage of the time, so too do the hymns.

"How Firm a Foundation," in a general way, is an excellent example of this characteristic. The entire song is about personal sanctification by means of God's Word. Established through faith in Christ—"who unto Jesus for refuge have fled"—we are reminded of "how firm a foundation . . . is laid for [our] faith in his excellent Word," and how such a foundation can "sanctify" us through any trial—sickness, troubles, foes, etc.

Another excellent, yet more specific, example (dealing with pride) is found in the first two verses of "When I Survey the Wondrous Cross":[14]

When I survey the wondrous cross
On which the Prince of glory died,
My richest gain I count but loss,
*And pour contempt on all my pride.*

13. In many post-1800 hymns, I also found this balance. "Take My Life and Let It Be" is an excellent example of this, for we sing to God to take our hearts, wills, voices, hands, feet, and minds—our very selves and lives—to be in service to the King. Another great example is Thomas O. Chisholm's "I Want to Be Like Jesus."

14. Another example, both of this fourth characteristic (practical wisdom) and the third (judgment), comes from the tenth verse in the original lyrics of "Jesus Shall Reign" (and, yes again, this verse is not found in today's hymnals):

The scepter well becomes his hands;
All Heav'n submits to his commands;
His justice shall avenge the poor,
And pride and rage prevail no more.

*Forbid it, Lord, that I should boast,*
Save in the death of Christ my God!
All the vain things that charm me most,
I sacrifice them to his blood.

The fourth verse also sings of our mortification of the love of the world (or worldliness).

His dying crimson, like a robe,
Spreads o'er his body on the tree;
*Then I am dead to all the globe,*
*And all the globe is dead to me.*

Other lyrics along this line include the following sampling, which sing (in order below) of our propensity to wander from God and his ways, our need for inward and outward holiness, our commitment, and our call to evangelism:

Prone to wander, Lord, I feel it,
Prone to leave the God I love. ("Come, Thou Fount")

Save from wrath and make me pure. ("Rock of Ages")

Make and keep me pure within. ("Jesus, Lover of
My Soul")

Take away our bent to sinning. ("Love Divine, All Loves
Excelling")

Let goods and kindred go, this mortal life also. ("A Mighty
Fortress")

My gracious Master and my God,
Assist me to proclaim,

To spread through all the earth abroad
The honors of thy name. ("O for a Thousand Tongues
    to Sing")

## The Contemporary Christian Choruses

One might expect, in keeping with today's emphasis on practical preaching, to find a greater percentage of "practical wisdom" in the CCC than in the CH. However, the top fifty songs provide almost no examples of this theme.

Other than "Change My Heart," which invites God to change our hearts to better reflect the character of God, and perhaps one line in "Lord Reign in Me," where the Lord is asked to rule over every thought and word, the other potential lyrics about practical wisdom are either too vague or too obscured by unbiblical or nonbiblical sentiments to count. Let me illustrate.

Although the Lord is asked to have his way in me (see "I Give You My Heart"), I am not told what his ways are (e.g., the command to forgive).[15] And while he is asked to destroy my darkness (i.e., sin?) by shining his gracious light on me, so my face might display Christ's likeness ("Shine, Jesus, Shine"), I am not told what that likeness is (i.e., holiness or kindness or generosity?). And while the virtue of humility is addressed (see "Indescribable"), and the act of evangelism is promoted (see "Days of Elijah"), such statements are neither prayers nor exhortations. That is, I am not asking God, in dependence on his sanctifying grace, to help change my thoughts, words, or actions.

15. In the first verse of "You're Worthy of My Praise," we sing of following God's ways. But again, an answer to the question "What ways?" is not found. Similarly, in "You Are My King," we sing, "It's my joy to honor you/In all I do, I honor you." But, again, how? How do we or should we honor God? By keeping his commands? If so, which ones?

Now, beyond the vagueness, a common "ethical" feature, not found in the biblical songs, is the theme of God's acceptance. For example, in "Mighty to Save" we sing of surrender to Christ after we first have sung of our Savior taking us as he finds us—with all our fears and failures. It is unclear to me if the "surrender" involves character change. I assume it does, but the lyrics are confusing.[16]

Other examples of what I call "character confusion" abound! In such songs, we are never exhorted to change. Instead, we are told to come *as is* before God in worship (see "Come, Now Is the Time to Worship") because we are, for some unexplained reason, called God's "friend" (four times in the chorus of "Friend of God"), and thus we can see our "beautiful" God (cf. "Beautiful One," "Better Is One Day," "I Stand in Awe," "Jesus, Name Above All Names," "Lord Reign in Me," "More Precious Than Silver") and feel God's warm arms wrap around us (in "Draw Me Close").

Whatever happened to the Great Commandment and the Great Commission? The heart of worship isn't my heart somehow blessing God's heart in some nebulous way (see "The Heart of Worship"), but rather is loving God by knowing and obeying his commands (John 14:15; 15:10; 1 John 5:2–3).

## The Twenty-Year Rule

Musician Bob Kauflin offers wise counsel with what he calls the Twenty-Year Rule: "If someone was born in our church and grew up singing our songs over the course of twenty years,

---

16. This is not in the top fifty CCC, but it is in the top sixty. "Mighty to Save" was listed at #2 in the CCCI August 2009 royalty payout, however.

how well would they know God?"[17] That is a very good question. Yet considering what we have learned, I would like to add another question: how well will our people know our Lord's commands and follow them? This is no peripheral question, for, as Chrysostom correctly comments, "The reason we comment on Scripture is not only for you to get to know Scripture but for you also to correct your behavior: if this does not occur, we are wasting our time in reading it out, we are wasting our time in explaining it."[18] It is time we stop wasting our time with lyrics that do not focus on the gospel and challenge us to walk in a manner worthy of it—in the way of wisdom.

17. Bob Kauflin, *Worship Matters: Leading Others to Encounter the Greatness of God* (Wheaton, IL: Crossway, 2008), 119.
18. St. John Chrysostom, *Old Testament Homilies*, trans. Robert Charles Hill (Brookline, MA: Holy Cross Orthodox Press), 3:43.

# PART THREE

## New Hymns on Old Texts

# 11

# Postlude and Prelude: An Introduction and an Invitation

*CWWO*

IN THE SIXTEENTH chapter of C. S. Lewis's *Screwtape Letters*, Wormwood, the minor demon, is counseled by his mentor, Screwtape, on how to deal with the fact that his "patient"—a new convert to Christianity—is now regularly attending church. Normally, this would present a problem. However, Screwtape recommends a number of "healthy" churches in the area—ones which would assist in tainting this new Christian's view of Christianity:

> At the first of these [churches] the Vicar is a man who has been so long engaged in watering down the faith to make it easier for a supposedly incredulous and hard-hearted congregation that it is now he who shocks his parishioners with

his unbelief, not *vice versa*. He has undermined many a soul's Christianity. His conduct of the services is also admirable. In order to spare the laity all "difficulties" he has deserted both the lectionary and the appointed psalms and now, without noticing it, revolves endlessly round the little treadmill of his fifteen favourite psalms and twenty favourite lessons. We are thus safe from the danger that any truth not already familiar to him and to his flock should ever reach them through Scripture. But perhaps your patient is not quite silly enough for this church—or not yet?[1]

Sadly, many Christians have moved beyond the "not yet." For today there are a lot of "silly" Christians. And part of the reason why (as we have learned in the last four chapters) is that there are a lot of silly churches which have a lot of silly pastors who allow a lot of silly worship leaders to select a lot of silly songs from a lot of silly songwriters.[2] And the result of singing songs that "water down the faith" and spare us "all difficulties" is the undermining of "many a soul's Christianity."

## Dancing with the Devil?

It's all very subtle though, isn't it?—the way Wormwood would want it. Instead of singing songs from God's Word, notably the Psalms, as has been the practice in Western Christianity since

1. *Screwtape Letters* (New York: MacMillan, 1948), 82–83.
2. Here I lay the blame first on the pastors, then the worship leaders, and finally the songwriters. That is, in my opinion, the order of blame. If pastors were better trained in music—in what constitutes a good text and a good tune—our churches would not be filled with such trashy hymns and compost choruses. I get the term "trashy hymns" from John Mason Neale, who used it to speak of some of the songs in the Breviary. See Paul Westermeyer, *Te Deum: The Church and Music* (Minneapolis: Fortress, 1998), 277.

Jesus and his disciples sang "a hymn" in the upper room (Matt. 26:30),[3] we are encouraged to take a step to the side. "Sure, sing the Psalms," the seemingly angelic voice suggests, "but just the ones you like, or just the snippets that best contextualize to our culture, or just the 'nice' parts of those otherwise troublesome dirges. So, yes, please belt out Psalm 95, but, for goodness' sake, bottle up its final five verses." Then we are told to move back a step, and there to turn up the volume and turn on the happy face—and turn away from that old-fashioned notion of rejoicing over judgments. "Remove that wrath" is the sensible, seeker-sensitive admonition. "No new 'Battle Hymn of the Republic,' please!" That's very patriotic, certainly. But such a song will be as fashionable today as wearing Lincoln's top hat.

Then the dance continues—two more steps, and we'll be done. "Turn to the left," we're told. "Now, take a big twirl." That's it. Yes, spin that story of salvation right onto the floor! People need to know what Jesus will do for them right now, not then. One last move—are you ready? "Come to a stop. Stand up straight. Feel the 4/4 beat. Let the chords—G, then D, and then C—sink into your soul. Now, raise your hands to heaven—and sing, sing, sing! Or better, shout, shout, shout!" The refrain is catchy and cool:

> God, God, God,
> It's all about us—
> Me, me, and you;
> You, you, and me,
> Oh, me, me, me.

My satire is not too far from the truth, is it?

---

3. "The psalm referred to in Matthew 26:30 would have come from the Hallel, a group of songs including Psalms 113–118, which was sung during the first two nights of the Passover festival." Marjorie Reeves and Jenyth Worsley, *Favourite Hymns: 2000 Years of Magnificat* (London: Continuum, 2001), 1.

# Ding-Dong Theology

Gordon Fee once said, "Show me a church's songs and I'll show you their theology."[4] Today's most popular songs—some of the CH and most of the CCC—show a theology that is un-Christian at worst and biblically unbalanced at best. Not only the texts, but also the themes of the songs of Moses, Deborah, Hannah, David, and Habakkuk are too often neglected. And such neglect has had its effect. By turning from substantive songs that well reflect these texts and themes to what Carl Schalk calls "Twinkie Tunes with a Ding-Dong Theology,"[5] a generation has gotten theologically fat and forgetful.

It is time we remove the Twinkies and Ding Dongs, and replace them with the milk and meat of the Word. God has given us so much to feed on. We are so spoiled with good food: We have 150 Psalms. We have the Song of Songs. We have the hymns to Christ, as well as other New Testament doxologies, benedictions, and prayers. And we have our six Songs of Scripture.[6] We have, if you will, God's "immense vocal score."[7]

You see, God has not been silent on singing. He has graciously given his church concepts and content for our songs. And yet we have so often sold his songs for red lentil stew (or whatever is now "hot" and brings immediate gratification). But instead, as God's children, we should claim these songs "as part

4. Quoted in Bob Kauflin, *Worship Matters: Leading Others to Encounter the Greatness of God* (Wheaton, IL: Crossway, 2008), 101.

5. See Carl Schalk, *First Person Singular: Reflections on Worship, Liturgy, and Children* (St. Louis: MorningStar, 1998), 81. This is the title of a chapter in his book.

6. And these are just the divinely inspired songs we find in our Bibles. I think we can even go beyond those. Pick any Bible text, "plagiarize" and paraphrase, and set it to song!

7. Paul S. Jones, *Singing and Making Music* (Phillipsburg, NJ: P&R Publishing, 2006), 26. Jones uses this phrase with reference to what medieval church musicians did with the Old Testament.

of our birthright," and celebrate them as "a significant part of our collective repertoire."[8]

## Sing an Old Song unto the Lord

The original song lyrics that close this book are my attempt to revive our repertoire. I have a love for poetic craftsmanship, an ever-growing appreciation for the hymn writers who have preceded me, and an earnest desire to be a servant to the worshipping church,[9] but I make no claim that my songs are worth singing or remembering. Yet in a day and age when so much "self-satisfied, unoriginal, and repetitive jingles" and "corrupting religious poetry" has gained a foothold,[10] where superficial and sloppy lyrics have become inadequate or even contradictory reflections of the rich and glorious gospel, this is a start. It is an introduction, and also, if you will, an invitation. It is time that those who are trained theologically, gifted poetically, and literate musically (and this should include a number of pastor-theologians out there)[11] write songs based on God's Word, even

8. Ibid., 99.
9. In his foreword to Christopher M. Idle, *Light upon the River* (Carol Stream, IL: Hope, 1998), Timothy Dudley-Smith writes, "To render the highest service to a worshipping church, the hymn writer must first be a servant of the Word" (p. v); and, "it is a weighty responsibility to put words into the mouths of worshippers" (p. vi).
10. The first quote comes from Christopher M. Idle, *Walking by the River* (Carol Stream, IL: Hope, 2008), ix; the second from Robert L. Dabney, who in 1876 "prophesied," according to D. G. Hart and John R. Muether, "the damages attending the triumph of contemporary music in Presbyterian churches." *With Reverence and Awe: Returning to the Basics of Reformed Worship* (Phillipsburg, NJ: P&R Publishing, 2002), 171.
11. "Seasoned pastors are especially well suited to hymn-writing, as a survey of Protestant hymnody readily verifies. Biblical learning, life experience, and knowledge of great literature and other hymns provide requisite subject matter, poetic models, and ample fare for allusion." Paul S. Jones, "Hymnody in a Post-Hymnody World,"

and especially the songs of Moses, Deborah, Hannah, David, and Habakkuk.

It is time the silliness stopped.

You may download original recordings of the following six hymns by Douglas O'Donnell, in MP3 format, for free from the *God's Lyrics* page on the P&R Publishing Web site—www.prpbooks.com.

in *Give Praise to God: A Vision for Reforming Worship*, ed. Philip Graham Ryken, Derek W. H. Thomas, and J. Ligon Duncan III (Phillipsburg, NJ: P&R Publishing, 2003), 253. Cf. Tony Payne, "Why Musicians Should Not Write Hymns," in *Church Musicians' Handbook*, ed. Sally McCall and Rosalie Milne, 3rd ed. (Kingsford, Aust.: Matthias Media, 1999), 109–15.

# My Strength, My Song, My Salvation

Exodus 15:1–21
Douglas Sean O'Donnell, 2007

MORNING SONG
John Wyeth, 1813

1. I sing un-to the Lord for he has tri-umphed glor-ious-ly, the horse, the rid-er, he has thrown in-to the blood red sea.
2. My strength, my song, my sal-va-tion, this is my God "the LORD." I will ex-alt him, praise him till his name be all a-dored.
3. Our en-e-mies went down un-to the depths just like a stone. But you, O God, have raised us up un-to thy moun-tain throne.
4. They trem-ble (all the na-tions do). They melt be-fore his fame. But we with one voice shout a-loud, "Our Lord will ev-er reign."
5. Has not the Christ so res-cued us, and saved us from the flood, of judg-ment from the hand of God, with hands that flowed with blood?
6. Great and a-maz-ing are your deeds. Let all the na-tions see. O Lord Al-might-y, just and true, to you we bow the knee.

# Why Should You Not Now Adore Him?

Deuteronomy 32:1–52
Douglas Sean O'Donnell, 2008

KIRKEN DEN ER ET
Ludvig M. Lindeman, 1840

1. Give ear, O heav - ens, hear, O earth, all of the words of my warn - ing. May they fall gen - tly, as the rain, soft - en - ing hearts which are hard -

2. Have you for - got - ten all his ways, how he has loved and re - deemed you? Did he not choose you as his own, call - ing you out from the na -

3. Do you not fear what God can do? Do not pro - voke him to an - ger. His sword is swift, his jus - tice true; he re - pays all who re - ject

4. He has com - pas - sion on the poor, all who are low - ly be - fore him. Those who choose life and heed his word, he gives all heav - en - ly bless -

ened.     Our God is   great,   a - bove  all   gods,
tions?     Up - on his   wings   he   car - ried  you,
him.     For he is   God   and   God  a - lone;
ings,     e - ven his   own   be - lov - ed  Son,

our faith - ful  Rock,  whose  ways  are   pure.
out from the  land   of   slav - er - y.
there is no  oth - er  like  the  LORD.
who for our  sake  a - tone - ment  made.

Why should you  not now a - dore  him?
Why should you  not now a - dore  him?
Why should you  not now a - dore  him?
Why should you  not now a - dore  him?

# God of Triumph

Judges 5:1–31
Douglas Sean O'Donnell, 2007

THREE KINGS OF ORIENT
John H. Hopkins Jr., 1857

1. See, O kings who reign from a - far, stars and light - ning march - ing to war. Moun - tains shak - ing, earth is quak - ing, wa - ter as weap - on flows.

2. Hear, O sons of him whom we sing, fix your eyes up - on God your King. Fear him, know him, bow be - fore him, bless - ing his ho - ly name.

3. Sing, ye na - tions, cry with one voice. Kiss the Son, O let all re - joice. He has shat - tered, he has scat - tered, dash - ing the e - vil foe.

*Refrain*

O, God of tri - umph, God of light,

God who con-quers earth - ly might. Strikes the strong with

his own arm. He lifts the weak to heav'n - ly height.

# Our King, God Does Exalt

1 Samuel 2:1–10
Douglas Sean O'Donnell, 2007

NEUMARK
Georg Neumark, 1657

1. My heart, my strength ex - ults in the Lord. My mouth de -
2. Talk not with pride up - on your tongues. Let not your
3. Those who were full are now left emp - ty, yet those who
4. The pil - lars of the earth are the Lord's, and on them
5. God guards the feet of all his faith - ful, but in the

rides mine en - e - mies. For I re - joice in
mouth speak ar - ro - gance. For is not God so
hun - gered find a feast. The bar - ren now have
he has set the world. Takes he the poor and
dark - ness e - vil falls. All of his en - e -

your sal - va - tion, for there is none so pure as
full of knowl - edge, weigh - ing all ac - tions per - fect -
borne forth sev - en, but she who bore is now for -
gives them rich - es, takes he the rich and makes them
mies are bro - ken, when jus - tice comes up - on the

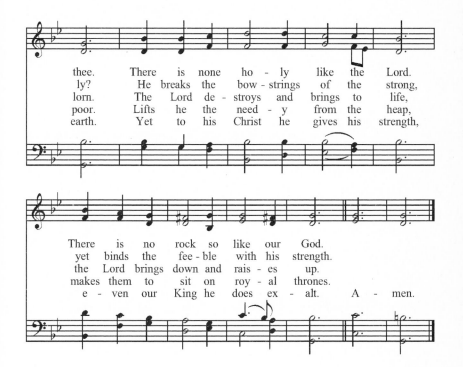

thee. There is none ho - ly like the Lord.
ly? He breaks the bow - strings of the strong,
lorn. The Lord de - stroys and brings to life,
poor. Lifts he the need - y from the heap,
earth. Yet to his Christ he gives his strength,

There is no rock so like our God.
yet binds the fee - ble with his strength.
the Lord brings down and rais - es up.
makes them to sit on roy - al thrones.
e - ven our King he does ex - alt. A - men.

# Though the Fig Tree Blossoms Not

Habakkuk 3:1–19
Douglas Sean O'Donnell, 2006

O WALY, WALY
Anonymous

1. O Lord, I know your might-y acts,
2. For once your splen - - - dor filled the earth,
3. So now we wait, O Lord we wait,
4. For though the fig tree blos-soms not,

and on these works I dwell in awe.
as it does fill the heav'ns a - bove,
and walk by faith un - til you come
and field and vine they yield no fruit,

And so I cry to you these days,
from low-est to the high-est height,
to con - quer all whose god is might,
yet I will sing with joy of heart,

these dark - est days, "Re - mem - ber love."
your light did shine, your strength un - veiled.
with your right hand, your glo - ry shown.
with heart so full, O Lord, my strength.

# Worthy Art Thou, O Christ

Revelation 5:9–11
Douglas Sean O'Donnell, 2006

LEONI
Synagogue melody arranged by Meyer Lyon, 1770

1. I saw a sa - cred scroll sealed with its sev - en seals
2. I wept, I cried, my Lord, for who shall ran - som souls
3. So wor - thy thou, O Christ, so wor - thy Son of God

with - in the right hand of the one up - on the throne.
from ev - ery tongue and ev-ery tribe to be God's own?
for through thy life, thy sac-ri - fice, thy church shall reign.

An an-gel's voice pro - claimed, "Oh take and break these seals."
Be - hold the Lion of Ju - dah! Now, wipe thy tears, his bride!
To God up - on the throne, and to the Lamb a - bove,

Yet none was found in heav'n a - bove nor earth be - low.
For Da-vid's Son, the Lamb of God, is cru - ci - fied.
be all our heart, mind, strength, and soul, our deep - est love.

# Appendix:
# The Top Songs Sung
# in American Churches,
# 2000–2008

I DETERMINED the top CCC using the CCLI database. This database lists the top twenty-five songs sung in churches per six-month period. I gathered the names and lyrics of the top twenty-five songs in each six-month period from 2000 to 2008, and then selected the fifty songs that were the most popular during those years.

In selecting the top twenty-five CH, the hymns met three basic criteria. First, the lyrics were written before 1800. Second, the songs are found in nearly all contemporary American hymnals, especially the best-selling ones. Third, over the last decade, they are the most sung in actual Christian gatherings.

For further explanation on my method and selection, see chapter 6.

# Top 50 Contemporary Christian Choruses[1]

| | Title | Composer(s) | CCLI# | Year |
|---|---|---|---|---|
| 1 | Lord, I Lift Your Name on High | Rick Founds | 117947 | 1989 |
| 2 | Shout to the Lord | Darlene Zschech | 1406918 | 1993 |
| 3 | Open the Eyes of My Heart | Paul Baloche | 2298355 | 1997 |
| 4 | Come, Now Is the Time to Worship | Brian Doerksen | 2430948 | 1998 |
| 5 | You Are My All in All | Dennis Jernigan | 825356 | 1991 |
| 6 | Here I Am to Worship | Tim Hughes | 3266032 | 2000 |
| 7 | You Are My King | Billy Foote | 2456623 | 1996 |
| 8 | Forever | Chris Tomlin | 3148428 | 2001 |
| 9 | Breathe | Marie Barnett | 785252 | 1995 |
| 10 | As the Deer | Chris Bowater | 871331 | 1987 |
| 11 | God of Wonders | Marc Byrd, Steve Hindalong | 3118757 | 2000 |
| 12 | Blessed Be Your Name | Matt & Beth Redman | 3798438 | 2002 |
| 13 | The Heart of Worship | Matt Redman | 2296522 | 1999 |
| 14 | I Love You, Lord | Laurie Klein | 25266 | 1978 |
| 15 | Give Thanks | Henry Smith | 20285 | 1978 |
| 16 | How Great Is Our God | Chris Tomlin, Ed Cash, Jesse Reeves | 4348399 | 2004 |
| 17 | Awesome God | Rich Mullins | 41099 | 1988 |
| 18 | We Fall Down | Chris Tomlin | 2437367 | 1998 |
| 19 | I Could Sing of Your Love Forever | Martin Smith | 1043199 | 1994 |
| 20 | Trading My Sorrows | Darrell Evans | 2574653 | 1998 |
| 21 | You're Worthy of My Praise | David Ruis | 487976 | 1991 |
| 22 | Majesty | Jack W. Hayford | 1527 | 1981 |
| 23 | Shine, Jesus, Shine | Graham Kendrick | 30426 | 1987 |

1. As reported to *CCLI United States* by churches in their Copy Activity Reports from February 2000 to August 2008.

| 24 | He Is Exalted | Twila Paris | 17827 | 1985 |
|----|---------------|-------------|-------|------|
| 25 | Change My Heart, Oh God | Eddie Espinosa | 1565 | 1982 |
| 26 | Holy Is the Lord | Chris Tomlin, Louie Giglio | 4158039 | 2003 |
| 27 | He Has Made Me Glad | Leona Von Brethorst | 1493 | 1976 |
| 28 | Above All | Lenny LeBlanc, Paul Baloche | 2672885 | 1999 |
| 29 | Draw Me Close | Kelly Carpenter | 1459484 | 1994 |
| 30 | We Bring the Sacrifice of Praise | Kirk Dearman | 9990 | 1984 |
| 31 | More Precious Than Silver | Lynn DeShazo | 11335 | 1982 |
| 32 | Better Is One Day | Matt Redman | 1097451 | 1995 |
| 33 | Glorify Thy Name | Donna Adkins | 1383 | 1976 |
| 34 | Sanctuary | John W. Thompson, Randy Scruggs | 24140 | 1982 |
| 35 | I Exalt Thee | Pete Sanchez Jr. | 17803 | 1977 |
| 36 | Lord Reign in Me | Brenton Brown | 2490706 | 1998 |
| 37 | My Life Is in You | Daniel Gardner | 17315 | 1986 |
| 38 | Beautiful One | Tim Hughes | 3915912 | 2002 |
| 39 | I Give You My Heart | Reuben Morgan | 1866132 | 1995 |
| 40 | Everlasting God | Brenton Brown, Ken Riley | 4556538 | 2005 |
| 41 | I Will Call upon the Lord | Michael O'Shields | 11263 | 1981 |
| 42 | Great Is the Lord | Michael W. & Deborah Smith | 1149 | 1982 |
| 43 | Celebrate Jesus | Gary Oliver | 16859 | 1988 |
| 44 | In Christ Alone | Keith Getty, Stuart Townend | 3350395 | 2001 |
| 45 | This Is the Day | Les Garrett | 32754 | 1967 |
| 46 | Days of Elijah | Robin Mark | 1537904 | 1996 |
| 47 | Open Our Eyes | Robert Cull | 1025612 | 1976 |
| 48 | Friend of God | Israel Houghton, Michael Gungor | 3991651 | 2003 |
| 49 | Jesus, Name Above All Names | Naida Hearn | 21291 | 1974 |
| 50 | Indescribable | Laura Story | 4403076 | 2004 |

**Top Five Contemporary Choruses: 2000–2008**

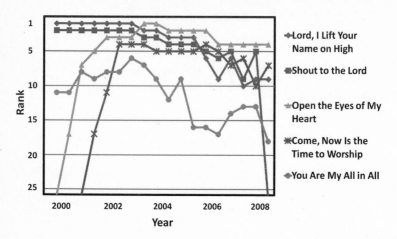

*Rank* is the measure of the popularity of a chorus according to the number of times the chorus was used, as reported by CCLI. Rank #1 = most used chorus, rank #25 = 25th most used chorus, rank>25 = not in top 25.

*Year.* CCLI has a six-month assessment period; one data point is included for each assessment period from 2000-2008. Assessment #1 = February 2000, assessment #2 = August 2000, assessment #3 = August 2008.

For more information about my research, including a table that ranks each six-month period for all fifty choruses, visit www.newcovenantnaperville.org.

# Top 25 Classic Hymns

## Pre-1800 hymns that are most popular in contemporary hymnals

| | Title | Composer(s) | Year |
|---|---|---|---|
| 1 | A Mighty Fortress Is Our God | Martin Luther | 1529 |
| 2 | Alas! And Did My Savior Bleed? | Isaac Watts; Ralph E. Hudson-*refrain* | 1707 |
| 3 | All Hail the Power of Jesus' Name | Edward Perronet; altered by John Rippon | 1779 |
| 4 | Amazing Grace | John Newton; John P. Rees-*stanza 5* | 1779 |
| 5 | And Can It Be That I Should Gain? | Charles Wesley | 1738 |
| 6 | Be Thou My Vision | Trad. Irish hymn, trans. by Mary E. Byrne; versified by Eleanor H. Hull | c. 700 |
| 7 | Christ the Lord Is Risen Today | Charles Wesley | 1739 |
| 8 | Come, Thou Almighty King | Some show as anonymous; others Charles Wesley | 1757 |
| 9 | Come, Thou Fount of Every Blessing | Robert Robinson; adapted by Margaret Clarkson | 1758 |
| 10 | Come, Thou Long-Expected Jesus | Charles Wesley | 1745 |
| 11 | Fairest Lord Jesus | Anon. German hymn; trans. source unknown; Joseph A. Seiss-*stanza 4* | 1677 |
| 12 | Hark! the Herald Angels Sing | Charles Wesley, altered | 1739 |
| 13 | How Firm a Foundation | John Rippon | 1787 |
| 14 | Jesus, Lover of My Soul | Charles Wesley | 1740 |
| 15 | Jesus Shall Reign | Isaac Watts | 1719 |
| 16 | Love Divine, All Loves Excelling | Charles Wesley | 1747 |
| 17 | Now Thank We All Our God | Martin Rinkart; trans. by Catherine Winkworth | c. 1636 |
| 18 | O for a Thousand Tongues to Sing | Charles Wesley | 1739 |

193

| 19 | O Sacred Head, Now Wounded | Paul Gerhardt; trans. by James W. Alexander | 1153 |
| 20 | O Worship the King | Robert Grant-*stanzas 1–4;* David Guthrie-*stanza 5* | 1561; 1833 reworked |
| 21 | Praise to the Lord, the Almighty | Joachim Neander; trans. by Catherine Winkworth | 1680 |
| 22 | Rejoice, the Lord Is King! | Charles Wesley | 1744 |
| 23 | Rock of Ages | Augustus M. Toplady | 1776 |
| 24 | The God of Abraham Praise | Thomas Olivers; based on Hebrew *Yigdal* of Daniel Ben Judah | c. 1400; c. 1765 |
| 25 | When I Survey the Wondrous Cross | Isaac Watts | 1707 |

**Sources:** Lyrics were obtained through two Internet sites—www.hymnary.org and www.cyberhymnal.org—and a number of hymnals, including these four:

- *Hymns for the Living Church.* Carol Stream, IL: Hope, 1974.
- *The Celebration Hymnal: Songs and Hymns for Worship.* Nashville: Word Music/Integrity Music, 1997.
- *Cantus Christi.* Moscow, ID: Canon Press, 2002.
- *The Christian Life Hymnal.* Peabody, MA: Hendrickson Worship, 2006.

# Bibliography

BESIDES THE BIBLICAL commentaries and hymnals referenced in the footnotes, below is a list of the most helpful resources for shaping my study of the Songs of Scripture, my theology of Christian song, and my growth in writing English poetry and prose.

Hauser, Allan J. "Two Songs of Victory: A Comparison of Exodus 15 and Judges 5." In *Directions in Biblical Hebrew Poetry*, edited by Elaine R. Folis. Sheffield, UK: JSOT Press, 1987.

Hill, Andrew E. *Enter His Courts with Praise! Old Testament Worship for the New Testament Church*. Grand Rapids: Baker, 1993.

Idle, Christopher M. *Light upon the River*. London: St. Matthias Press; Carol Stream, IL: Hope, 1998.

Johansson, Calvin M. *Discipling Music Ministry: Twenty-first Century Directions*. Peabody, MA: Hendrickson, 1992.

Jones, Paul S. *Singing and Making Music*. Phillipsburg, NJ: P&R Publishing, 2006.

Lockyer, Herbert, Jr. *All the Music of the Bible: An Exploration of Musical Expression in Scripture and Church Hymnody*. Peabody, MA: Hendrickson, 2004.

McCall, Sally, and Rosalie Milne, eds. *Church Musicians' Handbook*. Kingsford, Australia: St. Mathias Media, 1999.

Oliver, Mary. *A Poetry Handbook: A Prose Guide to Understanding and Writing Poetry*. Orlando, FL: Harcourt, 1994.

Proby, W. H. B. *The Ten Canticles of the Old Testament Canon: Namely the Songs of Moses (First and Second), Deborah, Hannah, Isaiah (First, Second, and Third), Hezekiah, Jonah, and Habakkuk*. London: Rivingtons, 1874.

Quasten, Johannes. *Music and Worship in Pagan and Christian Antiquity*. Translated by Boniface Ramsey. Washington, D.C.: National Association of Pastoral Musicians, 1983.

Rayburn, Robert G. *O Come, Let Us Worship: Corporate Worship in the Evangelical Church*. Grand Rapids: Baker, 1980.

Ryken, Philip Graham, Derek W. H. Thomas, and Ligon Duncan III, eds. *Give Praise to God: A Vision for Reforming Worship*. Phillipsburg, NJ: P&R Publishing, 2003.

Schalk, Carl F. *Luther on Music: Paradigms of Praise*. St. Louis: Concordia, 1988.

_____. *First Person Singular: Reflections on Worship, Liturgy, and Children*. St. Louis: MorningStar, 1998.

Tredinnick, Mark. *Writing Well: The Essential Guide*. New York: Cambridge University Press, 2006.

Watts, Isaac. *Divine and Moral Songs for the Use of Children*. Whitefish, MT: Kessinger, 2003.

Watts, James W. *Psalm and Story: Inset Hymns in Hebrew Narrative*. JSOTSup 139. Sheffield: JSOT Press, 1992.

Weitzman, Steven. *Song and Story in Biblical Narrative: The History of a Literary Convention in Ancient Israel*. Bloomington: Indiana University Press, 1997.

Westermeyer, Paul. *Te Deum: The Church and Music*. Minneapolis: Fortress, 1998.

Wilson-Dickson, Andrew. *The Story of Christian Music*. Minneapolis: Fortress, 1992.

# Index of Scripture

3:1–2—86
3:2—42, 92, 96
3:2–19—111n8
3:3–15—92, 93
3:5—96
3:8—96
3:9—96
3:12—96
3:16—92
3:16–19—91
3:17–18—112n9
3:17–19—86, 102, 121
3:18—146
3:19—71n2

**Matthew**
1:1—83
4:4—37
7:26—34
12:23—84
13:44—xxiii
16:26—39
21:9—84
22:37—80n8
26:30—175
28:20—43

**Mark**
1:15—48
4:19—38
10:17–25—38
12:29–31—40

**Luke**
1:26—82
1:30–33—83
1:46–48—83
1:46–55—7, 71n2,
111n8

1:55—93
1:68–69—83
1:68–79—111n8
6:20–21—38
6:24–25—38
11:31—83–84
16:19—38
22:19—33
24:46–49—48

**John**
1:1–5—121–22, 134n1
1:9–11—121–22,
134n1
1:14—122
1:29—142
1:36—142
4:14—25
14:15—169
15:10—169
16:8—155
16:11—155

**Acts**
1:1—135n3
1:7–8—48
7—138n9
7:34—14
13:16–23—84–85
14:8–17—123

**Romans**
1:5—44
1:17—102n22
1:18–25—34
5:6–10—60
9–11—42n27
10:9—121–22,
124n12, 134n1

12:19–20—156n22
16:26—44

**1 Corinthians**
10:1–14—161n8
10:13—32n11
10:22—32n11
11–14—118n1
12:2—134n1
12:3—121–22,
124n12
15:24–28—9

**Galatians**
3:11—102n22

**Ephesians**
4:7–8—136
5:14—121–22, 134n1,
147
5:15–21—118
5:18–19—118
5:19—73, 147n2, 155
6:24—80n8

**Philippians**
2:3–5—163
2:5–11—121–22,
134n1
2:6–11—163
2:9–11—147
2:12—45
3:19—37

**Colossians**
1:15–20—121–22,
134n1, 147
3:16—31, 73, 147n2,
161

# Index of Subjects
# and Names

INDEX OF SUBJECTS AND NAMES

Lutherans, xviii–xix
Luther, Martin, xvii–xviii, 9n7, 113,
    161n6, 164
lyrics, and melodies, xxiin6

MacDonald, George, 6
macro-salvation, 74
Magnificat, xx, 7–8, 83, 147
"Majesty," 129
Manichaeism, 141
Marcion, 5n2
Marini, Stephen A., 115n20,
    116n21
Martin, Ralph P., 122n9
Marx, Karl, 28
Mary, 7, 82–83, 93, 121, 147
McConville, 34n15, 41, 42
melodic line, 145
Mendelssohn, Felix, 156–57
mercy, 42, 60, 97, 101, 161
Methodism, 101
Metrical Psalms, 152
micro-salvation, 74–75
"Mighty to Save," 169
military metaphors, 9
Miriam, 17, 79n7, 146
mood, of song, 90
Moore, Thomas, 162
moralizing, 160–61
"moral songs," 160
"More Precious Than Silver," 169
mortification, 167
Moses
    last words of, 28–29
    Song of, xiii, xx, 3–25, 72, 79, 92,
        111, 121n6, 146, 147n3, 176,
        178
Mullins, Rich, 155

"My Jesus, I Love Thee," 139
"My Life Is in You," 129
"My Strength, My Song, My Salva-
    tion," 179

narcissism, xi, 142
Nathan, 59
Neale, John Mason, 174n2
New Age movement, 35
new covenant, 43–44, 147n3
Newton, Isaac, 11, 94
Nicetas of Remesiana, 30n10
Niebuhr, H. Richard, 148
Noah, 21, 61
Noel, Caroline M., 143n16
novelty, 35
"Now Thank We All Our God," 136
Nunc Dimittis, xx, 147

obedience, 39–44, 48
"O Could I Speak the Matchless
    Worth," 126n16
O'Donnell, Douglas, 178
"O for a Thousand Tongues to Sing,"
    167–68
"Oh Buddha," 94–95
old covenant, 43–44
Old, Hughes Oliphant, 151n11
"One Day," 137n8
"Open Our Eyes," 142
"Open the Eyes of My Heart," 129,
    142n14
oppression, 14
Origen, 8n3
Ortega, Fernando, 115n20
Orthodox Presbyterian Church,
    150n8
Otto, Rudolf, 92n7

208